Leckie×Leckie

Scotland's leading educational publishers

National 5
BUSINESS MANAGEMENT
SUCCESS GUIDE

N5 BUSINESS MANAGEMENT *SUCCESS GUIDE*

Anne Ross

© 2018 Leckie & Leckie Ltd
Cover image © tadamichi / Shutterstock.com

001/02042018

10 9 8 7 6 5 4 3 2 1

ISBN 9780008281700

Published by
Leckie & Leckie Ltd
An imprint of HarperCollins*Publishers*
Westerhill Road, Bishopbriggs, Glasgow, G64 2QT
T: 0844 576 8126   F: 0844 576 8131
leckieandleckie@harpercollins.co.uk   www.leckieandleckie.co.uk

Special thanks to
Donna Cole (copyeditor and proofreader)
Delphine Lawrance (picture research)
Q2A Bill Smith (layout)

A CIP Catalogue record for this book is available from the British Library.

Acknowledgements
We would like to thank the following for permission to reproduce their
material:
Car production photo on page 16 © Nataliya Hora/Shutterstock.com; RBS logo
on page 19 courtesy of RBS; SCVO logo on page 24 courtesy of the Scottish
Council for Voluntary Organisations; photo of high street on page 28 © Chris
Green/Shutterstock.com; photo of protest on page 33 © Albert H. Teich/
Shutterstock.com; photo of the Scottish Parliament on page 34 © Jeff J Mitchell/
Getty Images; photo of music festival on page 35 © Christian Bertrand/
Shutterstock.com; Ford badge on page 43 © Roberto Lusso/Shutterstock.com;
Cadbury logo on page 43 © chrisdorney/Shutterstock.com; Nike on page 44 ©
pio3/Shutterstock.com; Kits Kats on page 45 © urbanbuzz/Shutterstock.com;
Crème eggs on page 45 © Lenscap Photography/Shutterstock.com; Cereal
boxes on page 46 © defotoberg/Shutterstock.com; Apple iPhone on page 47
© Halfpoint/Shutterstock.com; Burger King/McDonald's on page 48 © www.
hollandfoto.net/Shutterstock.com; B&Q on page 49 © urbanbuzz/Shutterstock.
com; London buses on page 49 © pashamba/Shutterstock.com; McDonald's
on page 53 © Tooykrub/Shutterstock.com; photo of tea-picking on page 62 ©
Simon Rawles; FAIRTRADE Mark logo on page 62 courtesy of Fairtrade
International; photo of cans being recycled on page 64 © Huguette Roe/
Shutterstock.com; photo of lecture on page 72 © Pavel L Photo and Video/
Shutterstock.com; photo of protest on page 76 © i4cocl2/Shutterstock.com;
Monster on page 83 © dennizn/Shutterstock.com; photo of production line on
page 93 © Bartolomiej Magierowski/Shutterstock.com

All other images from Shutterstock.

ebook

To access the ebook version of this Success Guide visit
www.collins.co.uk/ebooks
and follow the step-by-step instructions.

Contents

Contents

Area of study 4:
Management of people

Area of study 5:
Management of finance

The Business Management course

About this *Success Guide*

This book has been written to help you succeed in the National 5 Business Management course. Throughout this course you will gain knowledge and understanding of business concepts, as well as an understanding of people and finance, marketing and operations. You will develop skills and learn how to apply those skills.

Throughout this book you will see Exam Tips, Develop Your Skills, Apply Your Knowledge and Quick Tests, as well as recaps of all the topics you have studied.

- Exam Tips have advice that should help you both during your course and for the exam and assignment. You should pay careful attention to these.
- Develop Your Skills sections help you to apply your knowledge and understanding in order to develop your skills in literacy, numeracy, decision-making, research and communication.
- Apply Your Knowledge sections are designed to get you thinking about some of the issues raised in the chapters. The answers to these sections are not always straightforward; you will have to think about the particular situation you are being asked about.
- Quick Tests are designed to get you thinking as you work through this *Success Guide*. All the answers are provided for you from page 96 onwards.

Course content

The course comprises five areas of study:

1. Understanding business

2. Management of marketing

3. Management of operations

4. Management of people

5. Management of finance

> **EXAM TIP**
>
> From the beginning of your course you should always use proper business terminology. It would be helpful to create your own glossary of business words and phrases.

The course assessment

The course assessment has two components:

Component 1 is an exam question paper that is worth 90 marks. This question paper has two sections.

- **Section 1** is worth 40 marks and consists of short answer questions based on stimulus material usually based on a real-life or realistic business.

- **Section 2** is worth 50 marks and consists of questions that require extended responses. There will be no choice of questions in this section. Questions in this section can be from any part of the course.

> **EXAM TIP**
>
> It is really important that you keep all your research findings organised, particularly when recording any websites that you have used. You do not want to waste time having to repeat your research.

Component 2 is an assignment worth 30 marks, which is 25 per cent of the overall mark. It is undertaken in class but is externally marked by SQA. The assignment gives you the opportunity to select an appropriate business topic, and to research and gather suitable information for that topic, which will enable you to make conclusions and recommendations based on your evidence. Once you have all the information, you will produce a business report which should be suitable for a business audience.

The course assessment

Introduction

In order to pass your Business Management course you have to sit an exam paper and complete an assignment. This chapter gives you advice about both. You can study for the final exam in a variety of different ways that suit your learning style. Some examples are given below. You cannot study in the same way for the assignment, but there is advice below on how to approach it.

How do I prepare for the exam?

Gather together all your resources from your Business Management course. It could be your notes, this *Success Guide*, textbooks, website printouts and class tests. Make a note of the main topic areas that you wish to study first. For each topic area, decide which study techniques you are going to use, for example:

- make a list of keywords
- use a mind map
- try a past paper question
- listen to a relevant podcast
- prepare a poster
- highlight notes and texts
- work with a friend on Q&A sessions
- use a website.

Decide on the time you are going to allocate to revising each topic, taking into account your own attention span. It is advisable to take short regular breaks and to drink plenty of water to keep focused.

The question paper (exam paper)

Section 1 has stimulus material. There are other names given to this, such as case study, passage, etc. This is usually based on a real business or a realistic business. The following steps will help you answer the questions.

1. Read the stimulus material carefully.

2. Read the questions to get an overall feeling for what is being asked.

3. Re-read the stimulus material and look for key business words or phrases that will help you answer the question. Highlight these if it helps you.

4. Answer each question in turn, paying attention to the command words.

Section 2 has extended response questions. These questions cover all the topics from the course. Highlight the command words in the question so that you are very clear about what you are being asked to do. Pay particular attention to the marks allocated to each question. Your answers should be as full as possible, with proper sentences. Bullet points are acceptable for some command words, which are explained on the next page.

Command words

The command words in the table below are examples of those used frequently in external examinations. You should pay particular attention to the command words used in any assessment you undertake.

Command word	Definition
Compare	Identify similarities and differences between two or more factors.
Define	Give a clear meaning.
Describe	Provide a thorough description.
Distinguish	Identify the differences between two or more factors. Remember to use where/but/however.
Explain	Give details about how and why something is as it is.
Give	Pick some key factors and name them.
Identify	Give the name or identifying characteristics of something.
Name	Identify or make a list.
Outline	State the main features. This needs more detail than just a list.
Suggest	State a possible reason or course of action (no development required).

The assignment

You will complete the assignment in class, and it gives you a degree of personalisation and choice. You should select an appropriate business topic to investigate. This will be your opportunity to apply the knowledge, understanding and skills you have learned throughout the course in order to solve a business problem or to advise a business about how to become more effective.

Once you have chosen your topic you will be able to research that business using a range of sources, for example:

- the company website
- other websites
- newspapers, journals and magazines
- advertising leaflets or advertisements on TV
- DVDs or videos from the internet
- field trips or visiting speakers.

Once you have gathered the information you need, you must analyse the data and come up with conclusions or recommendations about how the business can improve. What is important here is that you use your business knowledge in the context of the business you have chosen.

You will have to justify your recommendations. This can be the tricky bit as you have to be able to give good reasons, which are usually based on the following:

- Why have you made this recommendation?
- Is there an alternative?
- What will the consequences be if the business carries out your recommendations?
- What will the consequences be if the business does not carry out your recommendations?

Skills development

Skills for learning, skills for life and skills for work

Every course that you undertake as part of your education should develop skills that employers are looking for, and also skills that will help you progress in your life outside work. We all need skills in literacy and numeracy. In addition, we also need to be able to think for ourselves and to show that we are employable. The Business Management course will help you to develop a range of skills.

Literacy in business management

You can develop and improve your literacy skills in a number of different ways.

- Watching business news and making short notes.
- Reading about business in newspapers or on websites.
- Making a presentation about a business you have researched.
- Having a discussion in class.
- Composing business documents, such as job descriptions or advertisements for a product.
- Taking part in a role play exercise, for example a job interview.
- Compiling a business glossary.

Numeracy in business management

You can develop and improve your numeracy skills in a number of different ways.

- Calculating profits and losses.
- Preparing a cash budget.
- Entering formula into a spreadsheet for financial transactions.
- Preparing a chart or graph.
- Using financial information to make decisions.

Employability, Enterprise and Citizenship in business management

Everyone hopes to get a job when they finish their education. For some, this is straight from school, for others this is after further education. Whenever you hope to get a job, employers always look for certain skills. Are you employable?

The Business Management course can help you develop skills that employers are looking for. You will be employable if you can:

- show some understanding of how businesses work
- show initiative in your work, for example by undertaking research and solving problems
- communicate effectively both in person and using ICT
- demonstrate leadership skills
- come up with ideas to help the business improve
- protect the environment through recycling
- understand the laws that businesses have to work within, such as equality, or health and safety legislation.

Thinking skills

The Business Management course can help you to think about problems and how to solve them.

Employers want you to be able to think rather than just learn facts. We all have to think for ourselves on a daily basis, but in business management this can take many different forms.

- Using the correct business terminology.
- Researching a business problem and suggesting how to solve it.
- Planning, organising and completing business tasks.
- Working with others to link your ideas together.
- Using the internet with critical appraisal: Do you always trust the information on each website?
- Making decisions, giving recommendations and justifications.

Other skills in business management

The Business Management course will only be successful if at the end you can say that you have the ability to:

- make decisions based on relevant information
- communicate with others both in person and using ICT
- research, interpret and evaluate information to solve problems
- demonstrate enterprising skills and attitudes.

EXAM TIP

Skills are important in our modern society. For example, anyone can find basic information on the internet – it is what you do with that information that makes you enterprising and successful.

Satisfying wants

Needs and wants

Human beings have needs and wants, and these can be satisfied in many different ways. The most basic human needs consist of clean water, food, clothing and shelter. In the UK, people's wants surpass those basic human needs. People in developing countries are not so fortunate.

These wants include computers, fashion items, mobile phones, cars and holidays.

Businesses meet needs and wants by providing the products (goods) people are prepared to pay for. Some businesses also offer services, for example, hairdressers, restaurants, banks and travel companies. Once these goods and services have been used up then people expect businesses to provide them again. This is known as **consumption**. Businesses not only provide goods, services and jobs, they also generate wealth.

Goods can be classed as durable or non-durable. Durable goods last for a long time, for example cars, TVs, washing machines. Non-durable goods last for a short period of time, for example newspaper, magazines. Assets are owned by businesses and are used to help produce goods. Machinery and equipment are assets. Cash is also an asset which is used to purchase raw materials and assets.

The factors of production

Businesses provide goods and services by combining the four factors of production: **land**, **labour**, **capital** and **enterprise**.

Land	This includes all the natural resources of Earth, as well as the physical land where a business is located.
Labour	Men and women who make up the workforce of any business or organisation.
Capital	Machinery, equipment and all the resources used in the business. It also includes the money needed to start the business.
Enterprise	The idea behind the business, usually provided by an entrepreneur. Without this there wouldn't be a business.

Creating wealth

Businesses create wealth by adding value to products as they go through the various stages in the production process. For example, a carpenter who makes handcrafted wooden furniture could add value in the following way:

- the forest-owner sells wood to the sawmill for £30
- the sawmill cuts and treats the wood then sells it to the carpenter for £65
- the carpenter carves the wood into a table and sells the finished table for £150.

Throughout the process, wealth has been created to the value of £120.

EXAM TIP

Wealth is created by businesses adding value at each stage of the production process.

Apply Your Knowledge

Describe how wealth would be created in each of these production scenarios:
- Ford making cars.
- A hairdresser's business.
- BP producing petrol.

Develop Your Skills

Describe the factors of production in each of these business contexts:
- Making designer jeans.
- Producing a magazine.
- Building a new home.

Quick Test

1. Describe the difference between needs and wants.
2. Describe how wealth is created by a business.

Sectors of industry and the economy

Sectors of industry

The example of the carpenter producing the table illustrates the different stages that products go through, and these stages are known as the **sectors of industry**. There are three sectors of industry: **primary**, **secondary** and **tertiary.**

The primary sector

The primary sector involves taking raw materials from their natural habitat. These raw materials are then passed on to the next sector in the production process. Examples of businesses operating in the primary sector are farming, oil extraction, fishing and quarrying.

The secondary sector

The secondary sector involves taking raw materials and making them into finished products; this is often called **manufacturing**. Examples of businesses operating in the secondary sector are the manufacturers of products such as washing machines, cars, food and computers.

The tertiary sector

The tertiary sector involves providing a service. Examples of businesses operating in the tertiary sector are hairdressers, banks, travel agents, schools and dentists.

Sectors of the economy

As well as operating in a particular sector of industry, businesses and organisations also operate within a particular **sector of the economy**: the **public sector**, the **private sector** or the **third sector**.

The public sector

The public sector of the economy is owned and controlled by the Government and local councils. It provides services such as schools, hospitals, the armed forces and social services. These are funded by taxes. They are usually referred to as organisations or public bodies rather than businesses.

The private sector

The private sector of the economy is owned and controlled by private individuals and is made up of businesses known as sole traders, partnerships, limited companies, franchises, etc. They are funded by private individuals and shareholders.

The third sector

The third sector of the economy is made up of charities and community organisations that raise money for good causes and help people. The third sector includes social enterprises and co-operatives. They are not owned by anyone. They are run through donations from private companies and individuals, fundraising activities, and grants from governments, local councils and other public bodies.

EXAM TIP

It is important than you can distinguish between sectors of **industry** and sectors of the **economy.**

Apply Your Knowledge

Identify the sector of industry that each of these businesses operates in:

- Clydesdale Bank
- American Airlines
- Ford
- BP.

Develop Your Skills

Identify four businesses in your local area or an area that you are familiar with.

- What goods or services do they provide?
- What sector of industry do they operate in?
- Are they a large or small business?
- What sector of the economy do they belong to?

Quick Test

1. Name the three sectors of industry.
2. Give an example of an organisation that operates in the public sector.

What is customer service?

Customer service involves using a range of techniques in order to keep customers happy. However, keeping customers happy is not always an easy task.

- What does 'being happy' mean?
- Do all customers want the same level of service?

What keeps one customer happy might not suit another customer.

How businesses measure customer service

Businesses and organisations must have systems in place for receiving feedback from customers using their products and services. Feedback can take the form of **market research** or customers having the opportunity to submit their feedback via websites, customer service telephone lines, video booths, in-store comment cards, etc.

Why customer service is important for business success

Many businesses recognise the importance of good customer service and are therefore prepared to spend time and money investing in good staff and staff-training. If customers are happy then a business will benefit in several ways, such as:

- increased customer loyalty
- increased sales and profits
- a good reputation
- increased competitiveness
- increased staff morale and effectiveness.

Customers who feel they are treated well and receiving good service will be happy to return to the business. They will also pass their experiences on to others, which increases the potential of attracting more customers to the business.

Customer loyalty

To make customers loyal and therefore ensure they return to a business, it should provide the same standard, or a higher standard of products or services, at competitive prices. In addition, that business should regularly improve its products or services in line with customers' needs and their feedback. If anything goes wrong, a business should be proactive and take the appropriate actions to ensure that customers feel they are important.

Staff-training

The business or organisation must train all employees in customer service. Employees need to be trained to be sensitive to customers' needs and wants, and to know how to satisfy them. Many businesses approach this from a **quality management** perspective, and they may try and win awards for excellent customer service. Quality management means that every single employee in the business is trained in customer service and knows the importance of keeping customers happy.

EXAM TIP

Good customer service does not happen by accident! Staff have to be carefully trained to make sure that each and every customer gets the experience they are looking for and will return to the business.

How businesses maximise customer service

Many businesses and organisations maximise customer service by setting customer service standards. These often specify expectations, such as how long the telephone should ring before being answered, or how long it should take to answer an email or a letter. Another approach is to offer extras with each product being purchased, for example, by including free servicing or a car-wash every two weeks with the purchase of a new car.

The Royal Bank of Scotland (RBS) has created a customer charter that outlines specific customer service targets. It then publishes an annual report which states how they are meeting those targets.

The Royal Bank of Scotland

Apply Your Knowledge

What would you include in a customer care policy for a fast-food restaurant such as Pizza Hut, McDonalds, or Frankie & Benny's?

Develop Your Skills

Read the RBS customer charter at www.rbs.co.uk. Previously, RBS have stated that 'we will serve 90 per cent of customers in five minutes or less in our branches'. How do you think RBS can measure this? What will RBS do if customers are not served during this time?

Quick Test

1. Describe two ways that businesses can offer customers good service.
2. Give three reasons for offering good customer service.
3. Explain why it is important to train staff in customer service.

How to maximise customer service

Complaints procedure

Customers need to be sure that a business or organisation will take action should they make a complaint. Each business or organisation should have an established complaints procedure. This can take the form of a dedicated telephone service, an in-store customer desk or a feedback form on their website.

Refund and exchange policy

A returns policy will provide information about refunds and exchanges of goods and should contain the following information:

- whether the business gives refunds, exchanges goods, or offers other forms of compensation
- the maximum time after purchasing an item that refunds or exchanges are permissible
- the type of refund given.

All staff need to know the details of the returns policy and it should be easily accessible for customers. Customers should have confidence in the returns policy.

Guarantees

Businesses and organisations can offer **guarantees** to customers, but the conditions of these guarantees should be achievable and clearly explained. For example, airline companies cannot guarantee that all aircraft will take off and land on time, but they can guarantee the cleanliness of each aircraft and the approach to customer service adopted by staff. Guarantees can apply to the **physical condition** of products, for example, guaranteeing to provide a replacement if the originally purchased item stops working. Guarantees can also apply to **standards**, for example, guaranteeing delivery times for online purchases, or the qualifications of a driving instructor.

Apply Your Knowledge

What would you do in the following situations?

- A customer complains that their meal in the restaurant is lukewarm.
- A customer telephones to complain that their delivery has not arrived at the right time, and they have been kept waiting for two hours.
- A customer returns an item of clothing saying it is faulty, but you cannot see any sign of the fault.

Develop Your Skills

1. John Lewis has a policy called 'Never knowingly undersold'. Visit the John Lewis website (www.johnlewis.com) and find out what this means for customers.

2. Marks & Spencer has a 35-day refund policy for all items purchased. Find out what this means for customers at www.marksandspencer.com.

Quick Test

1. Explain the drawbacks of offering guarantees to customers.
2. How can a business make sure that customers' complaints are handled correctly?
3. What should a business do if customers are continually complaining?

Private sector businesses and local government organisations

Private sector businesses

The main types of businesses in the private sector are:

- sole traders
- partnerships
- private limited companies.

Sole traders

Sole traders are businesses that are owned and controlled by one individual. They provide the finance and run the business. Staff may be employed but the business belongs to the sole trader. Examples of sole traders are corner-shop grocers, hairdressers, and painters and decorators.

Partnerships

Partnerships are businesses owned by two to twenty partners. The partners provide the finance and run the business. Examples of partnerships are firms of accountants and lawyers.

Both sole traders and partnerships have **unlimited liability**. This means that if a business fails its owners must pay for all the outstanding debts and liabilities – even if their personal possessions (such as property and cars) have to be sold to achieve this.

Private limited companies

A **private limited company** is owned by **shareholders**. A company's name is usually followed by **Ltd**. Share ownership of the company is by invitation only, and the shares are not sold on the stock exchange. Private limited companies are often owned by families or friends, and are run by a board of directors. All the finance for the business comes from the shareholders, but those shareholders each have **limited liability**. This means that if the business fails then the shareholders can lose no more than the value of their investment in the company. Warburtons, IKEA and New Look are examples of private limited companies.

EXAM TIP

It is important to know the difference between unlimited liability and limited liability.

The table below illustrates the different types of businesses in the private sector.

	Aspect of business			
	Ownership	Finance	Control	Profits
Sole trader	Sole trader	Provided by the sole trader	Sole trader	Sole trader
Partnership	2–20 partners	Provided by the partners (but not always the same amount each)	Partners	Split amongst partners in an agreed ratio
Private limited company	Shareholders	Provided by the shareholders	Board of directors	Split amongst shareholders

Local government organisations

Local government organisations are 'owned' by the public but are controlled by local government (local councils). Local councils provide a range of services such as education, recreation and leisure facilities, housing and social services. The finance for these services comes from central government taxes and local council taxes.

Apply Your Knowledge

Carry out a survey of the employers of people you know. Do they work for a sole trader, partnership, limited company or public sector organisation?

Develop Your Skills

Search for businesses at www.yell.com. You can enter the name of a place and the type of business that you are looking for. For example, search for partnerships in Dundee and sole traders in Inverness.

Quick Test

1. Explain the difference between limited and unlimited liability.
2. Describe the ownership of a private limited company.
3. Describe how profits are distributed in a partnership.

The third sector, charities and social enterprises

Third sector organisations

The **third sector** is made up of community groups, voluntary organisations, charities, social enterprises, co-operatives and individual volunteers. The third sector makes an important contribution to economic growth and provides jobs and services across the economy. Third sector organisations are funded by grants from governments, local councils and other public bodies, and donations from private companies and individuals. Many of them use any profits made to provide additional advice, support and education.

The Scottish Council for Voluntary Organisations (SCVO) is the national body for Scotland's charities, voluntary organisations and social enterprises.

Charities

Charities exist for a variety of different causes. Some raise money to fund research into a particular area while others support individuals in crisis or difficult situations. Save the Children, Cancer Research and the RSPCA are examples of large, well-known charities.

Social enterprises

Social enterprises are businesses that trade to tackle social problems and improve the lives of individuals in their local community. They make money by selling goods and services, but they then reinvest any profits back into the business to provide additional support for the local community. Social enterprises do not make profits for shareholders – because they do not have any. Staff receive salaries just like any other business. Social enterprises can be food and drinks companies, arts, culture, sports and leisure centres, and business, financial and legal services. The Big Issue, Divine Chocolate and ASDAN are examples of social enterprises.

Enterprise and organisations

All of the organisations and businesses in each sector rely on their employees having enterprising skills. **Enterprise** is the idea behind a business or organisation. Enterprising skills can be developed by employees working in a business or organisation.

An entrepreneur usually comes up with the original business idea, and uses their skills and abilities to turn that idea into a reality. This involves not only taking risks and making important decisions, but also bringing together all the factors of production – land, labour and capital – in order for this to happen.

Most entrepreneurs compose a **Business Plan** before they start up their business. The business plan provides details of what the business will aim to achieve, and how it is planned this will be done. The business plan is usually structured to include key aspects such as name and aims, information about the product or service, the staffing requirements, financial planning including the necessary start-up capital, the proposed business premises, etc. The business plan is often presented to potential investors who may be prepared to provide the necessary funding for the business to get started.

Apply Your Knowledge

Find out about working as a volunteer in Scotland at www.volunteerscotland.org.uk. How do you think this differs from working in a business?

Develop Your Skills

Search third sector organisations at www.yell.com. You can enter the name of a place and the type of organisation that you are looking for. For example, search for social enterprises in Kirkcaldy and charities in Glasgow.

Quick Test

1. What are the main aims of third sector organisations?
2. Explain why an entrepreneur might start up a social enterprise business.

What are business objectives?

Objectives are goals or targets for the business to work towards. All businesses and organisations have **aims** and **objectives**; these are dependent on the type of business or organisation, and also which sector of the economy they operate in.

Businesses and organisations may also have a **mission statement**, which usually sets out a business or organisation's purpose and scope, what type of product(s) or service(s) it provides, its customers or market, and the area where it operates. Aims and objectives are an important part of the mission statement.

EXAM TIP

It is important to make a clear distinction between the objectives for the different sectors of the economy.

Private sector objectives

A major objective in the private sector (sole traders, partnerships, private limited companies) is **to make a profit**. However, these businesses may also have other objectives, including:

- providing a good service or quality product for their customers
- surviving in the market
- growing the size of the business
- having a strong brand that customers will continue to buy
- being the market leader
- being socially responsible by caring for the environment and reducing waste.

Public sector objectives

The main objective of organisations in the public sector is to **provide a service**. They use public funds raised by taxation to provide services at a local and national level. In addition, they aim to:

- meet the needs of residents, for example by maintaining roads and building leisure centres
- have a good reputation as a local council or government
- cover their costs
- stick to their budget.

Third sector objectives

The objectives of organisations in the third sector can vary. **Not-for-profit** organisations, such as community groups, volunteers and charities, have similar aims to:

- help those in need of assistance
- help relieve poverty
- increase access to education
- receive donations and grants
- promote their message or cause.

Social Enterprises that aim to make a **profit reinvest in the business** to help keep people in work. Alternatively, the profits can be used to **improve the social community** in some way.

Apply Your Knowledge

1. Research the aims and objectives of your local council. You should find these on your local council website.

2. Research the aims and objectives of your school. You should find these in the school handbook or on the school's website.

Develop Your Skills

1. Divine Chocolate is a social enterprise. Find out about the stages of production – primary, secondary and tertiary – from the Divine Chocolate website (www.divinechocolate.com/uk).

2. Oxfam is one of the largest charities in the UK. Visit the Oxfam website and find out about the vision, values and goals of Oxfam.

Quick Test

1. Describe two objectives of a private sector business.
2. Describe the main objective of public sector organisations.
3. Describe two objectives of third sector organisations.
4. Describe how a social enterprise differs from a private limited company.

Factors that affect a business: 1

External factors

Businesses are affected by **external factors**. These are events and situations *outwith* the business that affect its performance. These factors can be positive or negative. Businesses have very little control over these factors.

Political 	The Government can introduce laws that affect every business in the UK. Businesses have to comply with these laws and this may cost them money and reduce their profits. Examples of such laws are the introduction of the minimum wage, health and safety legislation, and corporation tax.
Economic 	Economic factors are changes in the economy during periods of boom and slump. If there is a boom in the economy then customers purchase more goods and services, meaning that businesses make larger profits. However, during a slump or a recession the opposite happens: customers tend to buy less since they have less money to spend. Businesses often cut their prices to attract more customers and this may have a negative effect on their profitability. More businesses go bankrupt during a recession.
Social 	Social factors relate to the structure of the population. Businesses need to respond to the needs of customers of different ages and also different working patterns. For example, over recent decades women have become a growing proportion of the working population, and this has led to an increase in childcare provision. Also, people are living longer, and therefore an increasing number of elderly people have needs and wants that have to be catered for. When the economy is doing well people want more luxury goods and holidays.
Technological 	Businesses must keep up with changes in technology. The introduction and availability of new technology enables businesses to create new products and provide new services. The use of the internet and e-commerce has revolutionised shopping. Online retailers such as eBay, Amazon and Argos have enabled customers to shop from their own homes.

Environmental 	All businesses face pressure (both socially and through the Government) to be environmentally friendly. Businesses have to reduce waste and pollution. They also are subject to the extremes of weather such as floods, storms, ice and snow. Extreme weather conditions may cause a reduction in business trading and therefore a drop in profits.
Competition 	All businesses face competition from other businesses in both the UK and from abroad. Competitors can attract customers by offering better products, services and prices. All businesses need to be competitive by lowering prices and by making sure that customers get the best deal possible.

EXAM TIP

External factors are often referred to as **PESTEC**. This can help you to remember the headings easily.

Apply Your Knowledge

Outline the possible consequences to a business if the following external factors apply:

- competition attracts customers
- the Government changes the law regarding the minimum or living wage
- the economy is in recession.

Develop Your Skills

The winters of 2010 and 2011 were particularly severe in Scotland, with heavy snowfalls and low temperatures. Research the impact this had on businesses operating in Scotland, particularly in the period just before Christmas.

Quick Test

1. Describe how the Government can affect the day-to-day running of a business.
2. Apart from bad weather, list the other environmental factors that can affect a business.

Factors that affect a business: 2

Internal factors

Businesses are affected by **internal factors**. These are events and situations *within* the business that affect its performance. These factors can be positive or negative, and businesses have some degree of control over these factors.

Financial	Businesses may not have enough finance to expand. They may also experience periods when they have to cut costs by reducing the number of services or products, and by making employees redundant. Wage rises, increases in the minimum wage or increases in the cost of raw materials can leave businesses struggling to make profits. Alternatively, when finance is available, businesses can grow and employ more staff.

Human resources	Well-trained staff are more productive and help businesses achieve their objectives. If staff are untrained and lack the required skills then this can lead to poor customer service and substandard products. Good managers motivate their staff to work harder and be more successful, but if managers are not properly trained then staff morale will decline and businesses will suffer. Businesses can also suffer if staff take industrial action.

Technological	Businesses will fail if they do not use current technology, and also ensure that staff are trained to make maximum use of it. Technology is expensive to install and maintain, and breakdowns can be costly. Technology on a production line includes machines and equipment that help to produce high-quality products. Information technology (computers, mobile devices, smart phones and tablets) has changed the way businesses operate and communicate with customers and employees.

Apply Your Knowledge

Outline the possible consequences to a business if the following internal factors apply:
- management are not trained properly to deal with employee weaknesses
- employees decide to take industrial action
- funding for new product development is difficult to source.

Develop Your Skills

1. Research how cafes, restaurants and bars can take customer orders using hand-held devices which send the order to the main order desk via a wireless network.

2. Research how online businesses such as Amazon and eBay can communicate with customers based on what they have previously purchased, for example, the recommendations sent to customers by Amazon.

Quick Test

1. Explain the difference between internal and external factors.
2. Give the actions a business must take if it installs new technology.

Stakeholders: 1

What are the interests of stakeholders?

Stakeholders are individuals or groups of people who have both an **interest** in and an **influence** on a business. Stakeholders can be either internal or external.

Internal stakeholders are people who are *part of* your organisation, for example:

- owners (including shareholders)
- employees
- managers

External stakeholders are people *outwith* your organisation, for example:

- customers
- suppliers
- banks
- the Government
- the local community (including pressure groups)

The table below shows the main interests of stakeholders.

Stakeholder	Interest in the business
Owners/ shareholders	The profits the business makes, since this determines the value of their share.
Employees	Their job security, and possible wage increases and bonuses, depend on how well the company is performing.
Managers	Their job security, and possible wage increases and bonuses, depend on how well the company is performing.
Customers	They want value for money, in the form of high-quality products or services at competitive prices.
Suppliers	They want to ensure their own profitability by continuing to provide goods to the business.
Banks	The profitability of the business, for which they may have provided loans.

Stakeholder	Interest in the business
The Government	They want to ensure that the business pays tax and obeys the law.
Local community	They want jobs for the local community, but they also want their local area to be safe from pollution and environmental damage.

Apply Your Knowledge

1. Think of the stakeholders for your school. What influence can they have on your education?

2. Who are the stakeholders in your favourite football team? What interest do they have in the team?

Develop Your Skills

Local council planning committees have to deal with applications for new businesses on a regular basis. If you were a resident in the local community where a new factory is about to open, what would your arguments be both for and against this?

Quick Test

1. Name two internal and two external stakeholders.
2. What interest does the local community have in a business?
3. What interest does the Government have in a business?

Stakeholders: 2

What influence do stakeholders have on a business?

Stakeholders can take actions that can positively or negatively affect the way a business operates.

Stakeholder	Influence on the business
Owners/ shareholders	Owners make decisions that affect the business on a daily basis. Shareholders vote at the annual general meeting (AGM) to appoint directors and influence profit-sharing.
Employees	Employees can choose to work hard and produce high-quality products and services. They can also take industrial action.
Managers	They make decisions every day that affect the business, for example, deciding who to hire as employees, which new products to develop, and the implementation of new procedures.
Customers	They choose whether to buy products or services and provide feedback outlining their level of satisfaction.
Suppliers	They can provide high-quality raw materials at reasonable prices. However, they can provide poor-quality products, and they can also increase their prices.
Banks	They can refuse to provide finance, which may put the business in a difficult position.
Local community	They can complain to the local council about the actions of a business.
The Government	The Government can pass laws at any time, and the business has to comply with those laws.

The impact of stakeholders on a business can be very important. Not all stakeholders will use their influences or take action which could affect the business. When they do, the impact can be positive or negative. For example, stakeholders who vote at the AGM can positively affect the outcome of the meeting. Stakeholders who actively criticise the business for its customer service can put off other customers.

Apply Your Knowledge

1. Who are Tesco's main stakeholders? What interest do they have in the business?

2. Who are the main stakeholders in your favourite band? What influence do they have over them?

Develop Your Skills

The Government regularly reviews the minimum wage paid to employees. Find out what the current minimum wage is, and what ages it applies to.

Quick Test

1. Outline actions that employees can take which may affect a business.
2. Describe the consequences for a business if they have to change their supplier.
3. Describe the main actions that customers can take if they are not happy with a business.

Who are your customers?

Every business needs customers, as without them buying goods and services, the business will fail. Customers have a wide variety of choice and will return to the businesses that they are happy with both in terms of the product or service and the customer service they experience. Businesses have to know who their customers are, and what their customers want. This can be done through market research and marketing activities.

Market segments

Businesses must know who their customers are and what their customers' needs are. Many products fail because the correct customers were not targeted. Customers are usually segmented into different groups based on certain factors.

Age	Products can be aimed at different age groups, for instance, young children aged 0–5 years, teenagers aged 13–17 years, or elderly people aged 50+ years (for example, Saga Holidays are aimed at people over 50).
Gender	Males and females are targeted with different products. For example, makeup is aimed mainly at women and aftershave at men.
Income	Luxury products like yachts, cruises and expensive jewellery are aimed at people with high incomes. People with low incomes are targeted by discount supermarkets, such as Aldi and Lidl.
Social class	Some products are targeted according to social class, for example, home furnishings, or leisure activities such as skiing.

There are other factors that can be taken into account when targeting customers, such as geographical location. For example, people living in hot countries need different clothes from those living in cold countries.

By concentrating on market segments, businesses can:

- adjust their products to specific requirements
- set prices to reflect the status of target customers
- design advertising that targets a particular market segment
- decide where to sell their products in order to reach targeted customers.

This is known as target marketing.

EXAM TIP

Carrying out market research is fairly straightforward. However, analysing the information, and then acting on the results, is more difficult and expensive for businesses.

Apply Your Knowledge

- Does everyone clearly fit into a market segment category?
- Do all teenagers want the same products?
- Do all people over 50 years of age want to go on a Saga Holiday?

Thinking about the answers to these questions should lead you to the view that market segmentation is not an exact science. People do not all fit neatly into a segment. Some people cross over many different segments. However, market segmentation is a useful tool for marketing purposes.

Quick Test

1. Explain why businesses need to know who their customers are.
2. What is meant by market segments?
3. Why is it important to target specific market segments?
4. What products would you aim at children aged 5–8 years?

Market research: 1

What is market research?

Market research is the name given to the process whereby businesses find out information about their customers and about the market. Market research involves finding out what customers want, but also finding out about what other businesses are selling, and for how much. Once this information has been gathered it is analysed, and decisions are then made about what actions the business should take.

Some of the decisions could include:

- altering the price of the product
- changing the product in some way
- launching a new product onto the market
- changing where the product is sold.

There are two main methods of market research, field research and desk research.

We will look at field research here and at desk research on page 40.

Field research

Field research involves going out into the market place and finding out information to help a business. This is called primary information.

Methods

Questionnaire and/or survey	This can be done in different ways, but basically customers are asked for their opinions or ideas. The focus is on how they feel about a specific product.
Consumer panel	A group of customers are brought together to discuss a product or compare it to other similar products. Their opinions and ideas are recorded.

| Hall test | This involves trialling a product with a group of customers; their opinions are recorded once they have tried it. |
| Observation | Information can be gathered by observing customers' behaviour in a shop; their behaviour is then analysed. |

Costs and benefits of field research

Costs of field research	Benefits of field research
Expensive to carry out.	The information gathered is relevant.
Time-consuming.	The information is accurate because it comes from first-hand experience.

EXAM TIP

Field research is important for finding out customers' opinions. However, what the business then does with the information is also very important.

Apply Your Knowledge

- How would you undertake a survey of pupils in your class?
- Would you ask questions of each person individually?
- Can you think of different ways to carry out your survey?
- How could you use ICT to help you with your survey?

Develop Your Skills

Use the Survey Monkey website (www.surveymonkey.com) to create a short survey for students in your class about their favourite ice cream.

Use the 'sign up free' for just the basics option.

Quick Test

1. Explain what is meant by market research.
2. How does market research help a business?
3. Why would a researcher carry out an interview instead of a postal survey?
4. What is the main benefit of field research?

Market research: 2

Desk research is the second method of market research.

Desk research

Desk research involves using information that has already been gathered by other businesses or organisations to help a business. This is called secondary information.

Methods

Government data	The Government publishes information from a variety of sources, for example, the Census or the Living Costs and Food Survey.

Printed media	Books, journals, magazines and newspapers contain information from a variety of sources about consumer behaviour and spending patterns.

Online research	There is data available online at business websites which can be used for market research purposes. For example, the Chamber of Commerce provides information about businesses and new opportunities.

Costs and benefits of desk research

Costs of desk research	Benefits of desk research
The information may not be relevant to your business.	The information may be free to obtain.
The information may not always be accurate.	The information is relatively easy to obtain.

Apply Your Knowledge

1. The Government conducts a census every 10 years in the UK. How can businesses make use of this information?

2. How do you know which sources of information to trust online?

Develop Your Skills

Access the Scotland's Census 2011 website: www.scotlandscensus.gov.uk
Read the section called 'Using Census Data'.

Quick Test

1. What is desk research?
2. Outline two methods of desk research.
3. What is the main benefit of desk research?

The marketing mix: product

The **marketing mix** is often referred to as the **4Ps** – product, price, place and promotion. Each of the 4Ps is unique in its own way but the combination of the 4Ps allows a business to develop a marketing strategy that enables products and services to be sold and profits made.

The first element of the marketing mix is product.

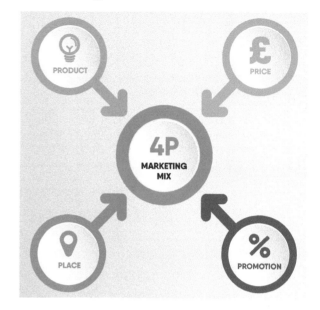

Product

This is the product or service being sold by the business. The product or service should have been developed in a way that the business is confident it will sell.

Products are launched onto the market after a careful development process.

1. An idea is generated.

2. Market research is undertaken.

3. Product research is undertaken.

4. A prototype is developed.

5. The prototype is tested on the market.

6. Adaptations are made on the basis of market testing.

7. The product is launched.

It can take several years to complete all of these stages. However, once a product is launched onto the market it follows a natural product lifecycle.

The product lifecycle

Most products go through a recognised cycle during their life. The product life can be short or long but the stages are the same. The stages of the product lifecycle are shown below.

Introduction: the product is launched onto the market.

Growth: once customers know about the product, sales begin to grow.

Maturity: at this stage, everyone who wants the product has already purchased it, and sales level out.

Decline: sales of the product start to fall as there are no new customers.

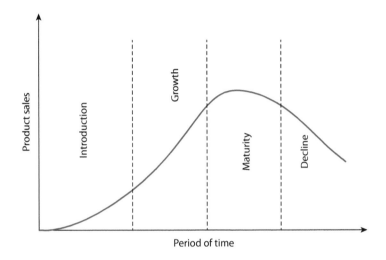

A business can inject new life into a product to try and prolong the lifecycle. This can be done by altering any element of the marketing mix, that is, the product itself, the price, the place where it is sold, or how it is promoted.

Product branding

A product that is a 'brand name' is easily identified and attracts loyal customers. A brand can be a single product or a group of products from the same company; for example, Ford, Cadbury and Campbell's each sell several products under the same company name.

Advantages of branding

Branding products in this way encourages customers to keep coming back because they know they are buying a product with an accepted level of quality. Branded products usually have an easily identifiable logo and a slogan; customers are often prepared to pay more if they associate a brand with prestige (for example, they may pay more for a designer t-shirt). Branded products usually enable a business to make good profits.

Disadvantages of branding

Some customers can be put off by the high prices charged. Also, if there is a problem with one product in the brand range, then this can affect all the products in the entire brand range. Some high-quality brands are also imitated by competitors, who sell the fakes as though they were the real thing. This can damage the entire reputation of a business.

Packaging

How a product is packaged can have a major impact on its success. Some customers prefer expensive packaging which gives the product the look and feel of a deluxe item. Other customers can be put off by expensive packaging which may be damaging to the environment if it cannot be recycled. Packaging can also help protect a product during transportation, so if the packaging is unsuitable the product could be damaged in transit. A business has to weigh up these advantages and disadvantages when deciding how to package their product.

Apply Your Knowledge

Find out how some businesses with famous brands have prolonged the lifecycles of their products by making changes, for example, Nestlé with Kit Kats, and Cadbury with Creme Eggs.

Develop Your Skills

Go to BBC Bitesize, National 5 Business Management. Under the heading Management of Marketing you will find nine class clips which will help your understanding of the various elements of the marketing mix.

Quick Test

1. Describe three stages of the product development process.
2. Name the four stages of the product lifecycle.
3. Suggest two ways that the product lifecycle can be extended.

The marketing mix: price

The second element of the marketing mix is price.

Price

The price of any product is important and sensitive to the demands of the market. There are a number of factors to be considered when setting the price for a product.

- What did it cost to make?
- What price are competitors charging?

The price of a product can also be determined by the quality of the product, the image that the business wants to project and the profit per unit that the business wishes to achieve.

Businesses usually adopt a pricing strategy based on the above factors. The most common pricing strategies are:

- **High price** – Setting a higher price for the product than competitors because the business is confident that consumers will pay it.
- **Low price** – Setting a lower price for the product to try and undercut the competition.
- **Cost plus pricing** – Based on the cost of producing the product. The manufacturer then decides on how much they want to make in terms of profit and add this on, usually as a percentage of the cost.
- **Penetration pricing** – Setting the price low for a new product, when there are already similar products, in order to penetrate the market. Once the product is established, the price will increase.

EXAM TIP

You should be able to name and describe pricing strategies and give examples of products being priced in different ways.

- **Price skimming** – Charging a high price for a product that is new and perhaps a bit different. Customers are happy to pay the high price since they associate the product with prestige or status; for example, the new version of an Apple iPhone.

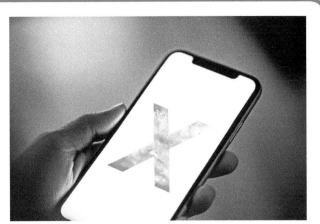

- **Destroyer pricing** – Setting a low price with the aim of destroying the competition. Once the competition has been destroyed the business can raise the price since there will be no other businesses supplying a similar product.

Quick Test

1. Name and describe two pricing strategies.

The marketing mix: place

The third element of the marketing mix is place.

Place

Place refers to how and where a product is sold. For instance:

- shops
- e-commerce websites
- markets
- TV shopping channels
- vending machines
- catalogues
- newspapers and magazines
- home-shopping parties
- telephone ordering.

Factors to consider when choosing a location

The location of a business is important. There are a number of factors that influence this decision.

- **Competition** – businesses choose to locate either near to their competitors or in a separate location. Locating beside competitors means that customers can make comparisons. However, locating away from the competition could mean that more customers will be attracted to a company's products.

- **Availability of resources/suitable premises –** businesses try to locate beside resources such as an available, suitably skilled labour force and good transport links, in suitable premises near to customers. Premises need to be affordable but also fit for the purposes of the business. In many cases businesses want space for customer parking, especially if customers are purchasing bulky items. Stores like Homebase and B&Q often locate in easily accessible retail parks for this reason.

- **Government assistance –** some businesses locate in areas where the Government is offering financial support. For example, in Scotland regional selective assistance is available to companies for locating in certain areas. Grants may also be available as well as low-interest loans.
- **Transport links –** some businesses consider locating close to convenient transport links, otherwise customers may find it difficult to reach them.

- **E-commerce –** when the location is remote, businesses often set up e-commerce options so that customers can order products online.

Methods of distribution

There are four main methods of distributing products to customers. Each of these methods has advantages and disadvantages.

Road – quick and direct to the door of customers. It is cheap and efficient. However, it can be difficult to transport large products, and there can be delays on roads at busy times, or during periods of bad weather.

Rail – useful for large and bulky items, or for very long distances. However, there are some areas in the UK where there are no railway stations. Also, this is not a door-to-door service, which may be unsuitable for some customers.

Air – suitable for small-to-medium products which have to be transported overseas. However, this is expensive and products have to be delivered to the airport, checked through customs, then loaded onto the aircraft.

Sea – suitable for very large products which need to be delivered overseas. However, this can be a slow process, and products still have be transported further once they dock at their destination port.

Apply Your Knowledge

Find out how internet sales have changed the way that customers buy products. Research this using news websites.

Develop Your Skills

Find out about Regional Selective Assistance grants for businesses to locate in certain areas of Scotland. Go to www.scottish-enterprise.com/services/attract-investment/regional-selective-assistance/overview; here you will find details of grants available for areas in Scotland.

Quick Test

1. Name the four methods of distributing products to customers.
2. Give one advantage and one disadvantage for each of the methods.

The marketing mix: promotion

The fourth element of the marketing mix is promotion.

Promotion and advertising

Product **promotion** involves persuading customers to buy a product using a variety of techniques; for example, money-off vouchers, discounts, Buy One Get One Free (BOGOF) and free samples. These persuade the customer into thinking that by buying they are getting a good deal.

Advertising involves transmitting information about the product. There are many ways to advertise a product: on television and radio, on billboards and posters, in cinemas, in newspapers and magazines, with flyers and leaflets, on websites, by email and text messaging, through sponsorship and celebrity endorsements.

The method chosen by a business will depend on the target market, how much money they are prepared to spend, what their competitors are doing, and what type of product they are selling. More businesses are concentrating on personal marketing – getting the message directly to the customer.

Ethical marketing

The increase in personal electronic devices has led to an increase in the number of people who can be directly targeted by advertising. However, not all individuals welcome this type of approach. Also, as advertising and promotion have become more sophisticated, there is a requirement to ensure that they are ethical, that is, that promotions are honest. Ethical marketing stops businesses making claims that products are going to change people's lives, and helps protect vulnerable groups.

Businesses need to ensure that their marketing and advertising does not discriminate against any group of people (for example, in terms of race or disability). This is called non-discriminatory marketing. They must ensure that their marketing does not mislead customers. For example, they should not make claims that products can perform miracle cures. They should also make sure that the language and images used in their marketing does not cause offense.

Apply Your Knowledge

Be advertising aware! Check out the different ways in which advertisements appear in your daily life, such as on billboards, at the cinema, on the sides and backs of buses. Can you remember slogans or songs and the products they are advertising?

Develop Your Skills

1. Check out prices in your local supermarket. How many special offers can you see? How many products have BOGOF offers?

2. Newly launched products get lots of attention. What pricing strategies have been used for tablet computers?

Quick Test

1. Give two methods of promotion.
2. List two methods of advertising.

Using ICT to increase efficiency in marketing

Technology has transformed the way in which businesses and customers communicate with one another, and the way in which customers shop.

Electronic surveys/social media

Electronic surveys are growing in popularity. More businesses and organisations are gathering market research information online. This is more immediate and cost-effective than sending out paper questionnaires to be returned by post. Online surveys don't usually take long to complete. They are often included as 'pop-ups' on a website, but can also be constructed on dedicated survey websites such as Survey Monkey. The results of each survey can be gathered quickly and analysed online. Electronic surveys can be used for customers and employees; employee satisfaction surveys can be conducted quickly and confidentially.

Electronic surveys can be carried out in different ways.

- Sending emails to customers with a link to a website.
- Feedback forms on websites and on social media.
- Sending SMS messages, asking for customers to provide ratings by text.
- Using survey websites such as Survey Monkey.

Businesses and organisations will continue to use electronic surveys to collect market research data.

Internet advertising/websites

Internet advertising has grown considerably in the last few years. Businesses can advertise via their own websites, but also through hyperlinks from other websites.

- A global audience can be reached on a regular basis.
- New animation and graphic techniques means that internet advertisements appear like TV advertisements.
- Internet advertising can be targeted directly at customers depending on what they are browsing, and links to QR codes can be added to social media sites.

- Customers can be reached in many different locations; for example, on tablets.
- Smartphones also allow customers to be targeted directly.
- Social networking sites provide opportunities to target specific groups.
- Customers can be targeted for recommended purchases depending on their previous purchases.

E-commerce direct sales

Customers have choices of where and how they want to shop. Online sales have increased considerably and this has had a knock-on effect on sales in the high street.

Customers can order goods online and have them delivered quickly to their homes, often with free delivery. Most high street retailers have websites with all their products available to buy online. They also provide secure online payment systems so customers feel secure when making online purchases. Similar guarantees are in place for online purchases as exist for shop purchases.

There has also been a growth in grocery shopping online. Most of the main supermarkets now offer online shopping with deliveries at prearranged times. Customers can do their shopping quickly on the website because their regular purchases are already stored, helping to speed up the process.

Apply Your Knowledge

What are the features of a good website? What should be included for customers' ease of use?

EXAM TIP

Customers can now make online purchases using a PC, laptop, tablet or smartphone.

Develop Your Skills

Have you completed an online survey? Was it easy to do? Find out if any members of your household have completed online surveys recently.

Quick Test

1. Describe two advantages of electronic surveys for a business.
2. Describe two advantages of internet advertising.
3. Describe two advantages of online shopping, for both the business and the customer.

What is operations?

Choosing a supplier

Manufacturers want to make sure that they receive good quality raw materials in order to produce their products. Therefore the following factors are important in choosing a supplier.

- The price charged by the supplier.
- The quality of the raw materials.
- The time it takes for raw materials to be delivered.
- The cost of transporting the raw materials.
- The reliability and reputation of the supplier.

> **EXAM TIP**
>
> Any delays in the delivery of raw materials will mean delays in production that may cost the business money.

Inventory management

Manufacturers can operate two types of stock-control system. They can hold stocks of raw materials in their premises or they can operate a just-in-time system.

Storing stock requires the business to have suitable warehouses or stockrooms. These must be dry, well-ventilated and appropriate for storing stock. They must also be secure to avoid theft. **Overstocking** can lead to cashflow problems if the stock is held for too long and goes out of date or out of fashion, or does not sell quickly enough. Most businesses operate a system of setting critical stock levels to avoid this.

- **Maximum stock** is the largest amount of each item that will be stored. This level is based on regular usage.
- **Minimum stock** is the lowest level of each item allowed before production could be halted, and customers may go elsewhere. This level is also based on regular usage.
- **The reorder level** is the level stock can fall to before a new batch of raw materials needs to be reordered. This is based on regular usage and the time it takes to order in and receive the new stock.

Understocking can lead to a loss of profit if customers go to other suppliers.

Just-in-time stock control

Some businesses operate a system of just-in-time stock control (or just-in-time production). Raw materials are ordered as and when they are needed, and they are delivered regularly to be used immediately. This avoids the need for expensive warehouses and stockrooms. However, it relies on suppliers being on time with deliveries. There can be problems during periods of bad weather or transport strikes.

Computerised stock control

The use of computerised stock-control systems allows businesses to have more control over their stock. These can be very simple spreadsheets which record stock going in and out and the balance; or they can be bespoke databases that allow management to closely monitor stock levels. Computerised stock-control systems enable a business to do the following:

- Print stock lists showing the balance of each item.
- Automatically reorder stock when a critical level is reached.
- Record details of suppliers and their delivery times.
- Automatically update stock balances after sales by linking to electronic point of sale (EPOS) systems.
- Update prices of stock quickly and easily.

Inventory control diagram

Businesses can use an inventory control diagram to monitor stock levels to ensure they do not run out of essential items. The diagram shows the maximum, minimum and reorder levels for stock and the lead time. Lead time is the time it takes for stock to be ordered and arrive so that production does not stop.

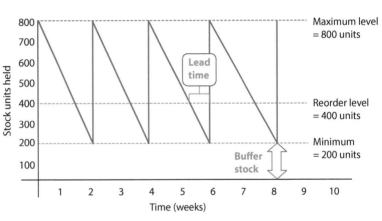

Apply Your Knowledge

Why do shops have sales? Why do they sell off their stock at a reduced price?

Quick Test

1. Identify three features of a good supplier.
2. Explain what just-in-time stock control means.
3. Explain what maximum stock means.
4. Describe the advantages to a business of using EPOS.

Production

Methods of production

There are three main methods of production – job, batch and flow.

Job production

This method of production involves a product being made exactly to customer requirements, such as a bespoke piece of jewellery. It is sometimes referred to as 'one off' production. The product is made from start to finish by a skilled worker, usually by hand. Because the product is unique, high prices can be charged by the producer. However, the labour costs of making the product may also be high.

Advantages/benefits of job production	Disadvantages/costs of job production
Products can be made exactly to customer requirements.	Products can take a long time to make.
High prices can be charged.	Bulk orders are rare.
Products are usually of good quality.	Labour costs can be high.

Batch production

Batch production involves identical products being made together at the same time. Subsequent batches are similar, although they may not be identical due to slight changes in the raw materials. Many food products are made in batches, for example, chocolate, crisps, bread and ice cream. The products are usually stamped with the date and time and batch number. They also have a 'use by' or 'best before' date. Other products that are made in batches include wallpaper and paint. Batch production involves both people and machines.

Advantages/benefits of batch production	Disadvantages/costs of batch production
Products can be produced more cheaply than job production.	If there is a problem the whole batch may be wasted.
Batches can be changed to keep up with customer requirements.	Machinery or equipment may have to be changed between batches, and this can be time-consuming.

Flow production

Flow production involves identical products like cars being continuously made on a production line. The role of employees is usually to maintain the machinery and intervene when equipment breaks down.

Advantages/benefits of flow production	Disadvantages/costs of flow production
Products can be made in high volumes at a relatively low cost.	Products are all the same with no individuality.
The use of machinery is efficient since it can run 24 hours each day.	If machinery breaks down, production will be halted.
Raw materials can be purchased in bulk, leading to cost savings.	There can be quality issues if quality control is not used properly.

Factors to consider when choosing a method of production

The method of production chosen will depend on several factors.

1. **The amount and type of goods being produced.** Job production favours small quantities of high-quality items; flow production favours large quantities where all the items are exactly the same.

2. **The machines and equipment available.** Some products require specialist machines and equipment, therefore batch and flow production are the most suitable, for example, cars and washing machines. This is referred to as capital-intensive production.

3. **The expertise and skills required to make the product.** Some products require high levels of skills and expertise, for example, wedding cakes and jewellery. This means that machines and equipment are not suitable. This is referred to as labour-intensive production.

Apply Your Knowledge

Flow production can be cheap and produces lots of products that are exactly the same – but what is an employee's role in this? Do you think they enjoy their job on a production line?

Quick Test

1. Explain the difference between capital-intensive and labour-intensive production.
2. Identify two examples of products that are made using job production.
3. Describe one advantage and one disadvantage of batch production.
4. Explain why products are cheaper to produce using flow production.

Quality

What is quality?

Quality means different things to different people. In terms of production, customers usually want value for money – they want quality that is consistent with the price they pay for the product. Products that are higher in price are usually better quality.

Quality products should be safe and fit for purpose. They should last for the period of time expected. An expensive pair of shoes will be expected to last longer than a pair of flip flops.

A quality product involves the following:

- using high-quality raw materials
- training employees regularly and to a high standard
- using up-to-date machinery and equipment
- using packaging that is appropriate
- the product being delivered on time
- the product being produced to a recognised high-quality standard (for example, the Kitemark system).

EXAM TIP

Businesses will produce products of good quality if they implement quality production systems.

Costs and benefits of quality

To ensure good quality, businesses have to be prepared to incur higher raw material costs, staff-training costs, and the cost involved in applying and preparing for high-quality recognition awards.

It is believed that in the long term the benefits of producing good quality items outweigh the costs involved in producing them. If businesses provide products of a good quality then they will gain the following benefits: customers will be happy with those products and will return to buy more; happy customers also enhance the reputation of the business; employees will be satisfied and better motivated; waste will be reduced; profits may increase.

Ensuring quality

Quality circles

Groups of employees meet with their managers to discuss aspects of quality. They may make suggestions on how to improve quality, or they may train each other on how to improve quality. The emphasis is usually on how to improve the quality of the final product.

Quality control

Products are checked regularly to ensure they meet the expected standard. If a product fails the quality check it is discarded or sent back through the production process. Quality control can be inefficient if it is only carried out at the end of the production process. It is more efficient to check quality at various stages during the production process.

Quality assurance

This involves checking products at more regular intervals during the production process and trying to avoid problems occurring in the first place. If quality assurance checks are carried out then employees can be more confident that the completed product will be acceptable. This reduces waste and increases employee job satisfaction.

Quality management

This involves every employee in the organisation ensuring that quality is built into every stage of the production process. It ensures that quality raw materials are purchased from reliable suppliers. Any errors or problems in the production process are eliminated and the failure rate of final products is very low.

All staff are involved in the quality process. Organisations often receive certification awards for achieving high standards, for example, Investors in People, charter marks, and the BSI Kitemark. These can also reassure customers that the product is of good quality.

Apply Your Knowledge

Do some customers expect higher quality standards than others? How does a business take this into account?

Develop Your Skills

Investigate any products that have been recalled because of problems in production, for example, horsemeat in products from major retailers in 2013. How could this have happened?

Quick Test

1. Describe two features of a quality product.
2. Describe quality assurance.
3. Describe quality management.
4. List the benefits to a business of selling products of good quality.

What are ethical and environmental issues?: 1

Ethical and environmental issues concern how businesses behave attempting to achieve their objectives. Trying to make profits in a competitive marketplace is not always easy, and businesses have expenses to pay. Some may be tempted to reduce costs by adopting unethical practices and neglecting the environment.

Producing in an ethical way

Some businesses pick suppliers who produce or obtain raw materials in an ethical way. For example, the growth of fairtrade products helps farmers and workers in the developing world get a fair deal. Raw materials may be selected because they have been grown organically, or that they haven't been genetically modified. Suppliers may be chosen on the basis that no child workers are involved in production, or that employees are given a fair wage.

The FAIRTRADE Mark is an independent certification label owned by Fairtrade International. When you see it on products it means that farmers and workers in developing countries have received a fair and stable price for their produce, and that the Fairtrade premium, an additional sum of money which goes into a communal fund for workers and farmers to use, has been paid.

Businesses may also select suppliers on how they manage health and safety matters in the workplace. If a supplier neglects or ignores health and safety legislation then they risk being fined or even closed down by Health and Safety officers.

If businesses import cheap raw materials or products from abroad then they may risk losing customers who believe that cheap imports are poor quality products, or because of a belief that UK employees are being replaced by employees working overseas.

The environment

EXAM TIP

Many businesses are marketing their products as 'environmentally friendly' to try and win more customers.

Different governments have actively encouraged environmental awareness. Businesses and individuals have been educated about the main environmental issues.

- **Waste** – businesses produce waste but this cannot be dumped, particularly if it is dangerous or harmful. Businesses have to find ways to reduce waste, and to recycle and/or dispose of it in a responsible way.
- **Emissions** – greenhouse gas emissions must be reduced to prevent damaging the environment. Responsible businesses use filters and screens to reduce their smoke and chemical emissions.
- **Sustainable development** – all production processes use raw materials taken from the planet. Some businesses operate a policy of sustainable development, in which they replace raw materials that they are using. For example, trees are replanted regularly to ensure future supplies of timber.

Apply Your Knowledge

Have you purchased Fairtrade products in the supermarket? Why do you think customers buy Fairtrade products? Are Fairtrade products of a similar standard to other products?

Develop Your Skills

Go to www.fairtrade.org.uk and find out more about Fairtrade products available in the UK.

Quick Test

1. Explain why it is important for businesses to choose an environmentally friendly supplier.
2. Give two main ways in which the environment can be damaged.
3. What is sustainable development?

What are ethical and environmental issues?: 2

Recycling and packaging

Recycling

Households and businesses recycle waste and packaging. Recycling is important and has several advantages:

- Waste materials can be made into new products. This means that fewer of the planet's natural resources are required.
- Recycled materials can lower costs throughout the production process by reducing the need for new raw materials.
- Recycling reduces greenhouse gas emissions from landfills and incinerators.
- There is less need to mine and quarry for new raw materials.
- If waste materials are recycled then fewer landfill sites are required, saving rural land space.

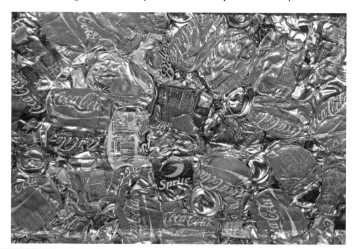

Costs of recycling	Benefits of recycling
Recycling bins and bags.	Protection of natural resources.
Paying recycling firms to collect recycled items.	Energy savings.
Transporting recycled material to recycling plants and sites.	Protection of the environment.
Building and maintaining recycling plants and sites.	Fewer landfill sites.

Packaging

Packaging is an important aspect of production in most businesses. Packaging helps protect the final product during transportation, and also on the shelves in shops. Packaging can help sell a product if it is a luxury item like perfume.

The popularity of fast-food outlets and home deliveries has increased the need for packaging, which not only uses up natural resources, but can also result in littering.

Packaging has been reduced for many household goods.

Costs of reducing packaging	Benefits of reducing packaging
Products may get damaged on route to customers.	Less waste and fewer natural resources are used up.
Customers may think the products are inferior without attractive packaging.	Less litter is dumped.

Apply Your Knowledge

Use the following websites to help you with the questions below:

www.recyclenow.com

www.greenchoices.org

1. What steps have businesses taken to reduce packaging and to recycle more waste?

2. Research some products which use excess packaging.

Develop Your Skills

1. What advice would you give to your family about purchasing products with packaging?

2. What advice would you give to your family about recycling in your household?

Quick Test

1. Give two costs and two benefits of recycling.

2. Give one cost and one benefit of reducing packaging.

Using ICT to increase efficiency in operations

Technology in business is constantly changing. Businesses have to keep up with developments to stay competitive and meet customers' needs.

Computer-aided design (CAD)

CAD is the name given to software programs that allow the user to create drawings, plans and blueprints using computers. Previously, these would have been done by hand. Architects, graphic designers and engineers produce drawings and plans in 2D and 3D that allow customers to see images of what the final product will look like. This could be a new kitchen, a new house, or an electrical product.

Computer-aided manufacture (CAM)

CAM is the name given to manufacturing systems that are automated. The machinery and robots used in the production process are controlled by a computer. The computer gives instructions that can be changed at short notice if necessary, or can facilitate small changes in the design. The use of CAM allows precision in the manufacturing process and it also reduces the number of employees required.

EXAM TIP

You must be able to describe how the technology used improves how the business operates.

Electronic point of sale (EPOS)

EPOS is also known as an electronic checkout. Large stores and supermarkets use EPOS at the sales point or checkout when customers purchase goods and/or services. The EPOS system scans the barcode on the item being bought then deducts that item from the total stock balance. This allows a business to accurately track their stock levels of every item. At the end of each day's trading a list of all the stock items sold that day can be printed out. Most EPOS systems use touch screens, which speeds up transactions with customers.

EPOS can gather valuable data which can be used for market research. The data can also help produce reports showing which items have sold quickly and those items which are are not so popular. Prices can be changed at any time on an EPOS system, so businesses can track how sensitive demand is to price changes.

Apply Your Knowledge

EPOS has changed the way retailers operate but how does it improve the experience for customers?

Develop Your Skills

Examine products you have bought recently. Can you see the barcode information?

- What does the business do with barcode information?
- How does this help their stock control?

Quick Test

1. Give a description of CAD.
2. Give a description of CAM.
3. Explain EPOS and how it helps with stock control.

Recruitment

Recruitment is the process of getting potential candidates to apply for a job vacancy.

Recruitment methods

Recruitment can be conducted **internally** or **externally**. With internal recruitment, job vacancies are filled by existing staff. The vacancies are advertised internally and applicants are interviewed if they are suitable. Vacancies can also be filled by promoting employees (perhaps after appraisal interviews).

With external recruitment, a vacancy is filled by a process of open competition. Existing employees can apply but vacancies are advertised externally and applications are invited from outwith the organisation.

Stages of the recruitment process

EXAM TIP

It is important to know the difference between a job description, which is about the job itself, and a person specification, which is about the type of person the business is looking for to fill the job.

Each business or organisation will go through a series of stages in order to recruit the best candidate.

Identifying the job vacancy
This means making sure that the job vacancy exists, and the reasons why.

Conducting a job analysis
This involves identifying in more detail what the role actually involves. What are the tasks and duties that will be carried out in the job?

Preparing a job description
A job description is a detailed account of the job. This is usually sent to applicants for the vacancy to help them check this is a suitable job for them. The job description will include the job title, the duties and responsibilities, the location of the job, and the terms and conditions including the salary, annual leave entitlement and pension entitlement.

Preparing a person specification
A person specification is prepared after the job analysis has been completed. It provides details of the type of person the business is looking for to do the job. The person specification includes essential and desirable attributes: **essential** means the applicant must have them and **desirable** means it would be advantageous if they did have them. The person specification might ask for skills, qualities, qualifications, relevant experience and any additional requirements, for instance a driving licence.

Advertising the vacancy internally and externally

Job vacancies can be advertised in a variety of ways such as in newspapers and magazines, on websites, and in job centres.

Alternatively, the business may pay for a **recruitment agency** to find them suitable candidates. The agency take responsibility for advertising the job vacancy, pre-screening and shortlisting candidates. This is helpful if a business is small and does not have the expertise or resources for recruiting. Larger businesses also use recruitment agencies because it is less time-consuming.

Application forms and CVs

Each applicant can be sent out an application form to complete and return, or the application form can be completed online. Application forms are useful because the business receives information in the same format from each candidate.

Some businesses may ask candidates to send their CV instead of completing an application form. A CV is a summary of a candidate's skills, abilities, relevant work experience and qualifications. CVs are usually prepared by each candidate; a strong CV increases a candidate's chances of being invited for interview.

Businesses may also ask candidates for a reference from their current or most recent employer. The reference should state the skills of the candidate and how they performed in their current or most recent job.

Apply Your Knowledge

Describe the benefits to a business of candidates completing online application forms, and the advantages to candidates of sending in a CV.

Develop Your Skills

Visit www.s1jobs.com to see the wide variety of jobs that are advertised across Scotland each day. What information do employers give?

Quick Test

1. Compare internal and external recruitment.
2. Identify three pieces of information contained in a job description.
3. Describe what a recruitment agency would use a person specification for.
4. Identify three places where jobs can be advertised externally.

Selection of employees

The selection process

Once all the applications and/or CVs have been received from candidates, the selection process begins to find the best person to fill the job vacancy.

The business goes through all the candidates checking to see who meets the essential attributes listed in the person specification for the vacancy. Those who do have the essential attributes, and more desirable attributes than other candidates, are invited to take part in one of many different selection methods. The selection process may take place at the business itself, or at an assessment centre (which could be located at a recruitment agency).

EXAM TIP

It is important that businesses match the candidates' applications with the person specification otherwise they will find it difficult to reject applications.

Selection methods

The interview

Before the interviews the business selects an interview panel, and decides where and when the interviews will take place. They also prepare suitable questions to ask the candidates.

During the interview the panel will make notes on what each candidate says so that they can assess and compare the answers from the candidates once all the interviews have taken place.

In order to assist with the selection, the panel should also consider references from previous employers. References or referees provide a report on the applicant to back up their application. This will normally state how reliable, honest and suitable the candidate is for the job.

Once the interview panel have assessed all the candidates and made a decision their preferred candidate will be offered the job subject to satisfactory references.

Giving a presentation

Candidates may be asked to give a presentation to the panel. This could involve a PowerPoint presentation using a computer or a flipchart with marker pens.

Role play

Candidates may be asked to take part in a role play that shows how they react in different situations, for instance dealing with a difficult customer. The scenario is designed to show the strengths, weaknesses and personalities of the candidates.

Group discussions

Candidates may be asked to take part in a discussion with the other shortlisted candidates. This is designed to show the leadership and interpersonal skills of the candidates.

Team-building tasks

Candidates may be asked to work as part of a team to solve a particular problem. They are assessed on how well they work together to deliver a satisfactory solution. This also provides an insight into the leadership and interpersonal skills each candidate has.

Personality or aptitude tests

These usually take place along with one or more of the other types of selection method. For example, the candidate may sit the personality or aptitude test after their interview. These tests assess the knowledge, ability and personality of each candidate. Many of these tests are now conducted online.

Apply Your Knowledge

1. What information would a business need to give to an assessment centre before applicants sat selection tests for a job?

2. Prepare three interview questions for the post of Customer Service Manager.

3. Can you accurately assess a candidate who has kept quiet during a group discussion?

Develop Your Skills

1. What would you include in a team-building task for the post of Marketing Assistant?

2. How important is the appearance of the candidate at an interview?

3. What leadership skills are employers looking for in a group discussion task?

Quick Test

1. Give the advantages of using an interview as the only means of selecting a candidate for a job.

2. Describe the disadvantages of using personality tests as a means of selecting candidates.

3. Describe the role a recruitment agency plays in the recruitment process.

Training of employees

Types of training

EXAM TIP

You should be able to distinguish between on-the-job and off-the-job training.

- **On-the-job training** is carried out in the workplace. It is undertaken by employees to improve their knowledge, skills and performance at work.

- **Off-the-job training** is carried out away from the workplace. It can be undertaken at a college, university or training centre. It may involve studying for additional qualifications. The training is usually delivered by experts in a particular field.

- **Induction training** is usually carried out in the workplace. It is given to new employees and can include training about the wider business sector as well as specific training related to the job. Induction training usually also includes health and safety issues, arrangements for signing in and out, how to book holidays, the absence notification procedure, etc.

Methods of training

Whichever type of training is undertaken, it can be carried out in a variety of ways which suit business, the employees, or the product or service the organisation provides.

- **Lectures** are often used for off-the-job training to reach large numbers of people at the same time. They are a useful way of giving out information.

- **Role playing and simulation** enable employees to show how they solve issues with customers or deal with other colleagues. Employees are asked to play out different scenarios and to learn from them.

- **Job rotation** involves employees working their way through a series of different jobs so they become acquainted with the different tasks and responsibilities associated with different roles.

- **Apprenticeships** are appropriate for jobs requiring mechanical skills, for example plumbing and engineering. Apprenticeships are also available in administration and finance.

- **Multimedia** training has a variety of forms, for instance DVDs, PowerPoint presentations, films and computer simulations. Some of these can be undertaken by the employee in their own time.

Costs and benefits of training

Training employees can be expensive, so businesses have to weigh up the costs and benefits to make sure it is worthwhile.

Type of Training	Costs	Benefits
On-the-job	• Employees are unable to work while being trained. • Employees may feel awkward being trained by each other.	• Training is specific to the job. • No time is lost spent travelling to and from the training venue.
Off-the-job	• Employees spend time away from the workplace. • The cost of training can be high.	• Training is carried out by experts so should be of a good quality. • Employees can be motivated by the prospect of gaining additional qualifications.

Apply Your Knowledge

1. What elements would you include in an induction training programme for a new teacher at your school?

2. What training or teaching methods do you experience at school each day? Which of these do you enjoy the most?

Develop Your Skills

How would you persuade an employee to undertake a training programme that took them 'off-the-job'?

Quick Test

1. Explain the difference between on-the-job and off-the-job training.
2. Describe two costs and two benefits of on-the-job training.
3. Describe two methods of employee training that could be off-the-job.
4. Describe what induction training is.

Motivating and retaining employees

Motivating staff

Employers want to keep their employees happy. If employees are happy they are more likely to perform well and remain with the business.

Financial rewards

The way employees are paid varies.

- **Time rates** – employees are paid hourly. Different jobs have different hourly rates. The Government sets a minimum hourly wage, which is the least amount that must be paid to employees.
- **Piece rates** – employees are paid according to the amount they produce. This has to be measured. If employees work harder and produce more then they earn more.
- **Wage/salary (flat rate)** – employees are paid an agreed amount every week or month. The wage or salary does not usually change, and it is not related to the amount they produce or sell.
- **Overtime** – time worked outwith the usual working hours. Overtime could be paid at one-and-a-half times or at double the employee's regular hourly rate.
- **Bonus** – bonuses are paid in addition to the regular wage or salary for a variety of reasons; for example, meeting a specific sales target or producing the most goods.

Non-financial rewards

These are other ways of rewarding staff which do not involve direct payments. These are often called 'perks'.

- **Company car** – the business provides a car for the employee to use.
- **Pension/insurance** – some employers make enhanced contributions to employees' retirement pension funds (exceeding the legally stipulated minimum). Some employers also provide medical insurance or travel insurance for their employees.
- **Luncheon vouchers/subsidised canteen/staff discount** – some employers pay for lunches or provide canteen facilities where employees can buy meals at reduced prices. Many large retail companies offer their staff a discount on goods purchased.
- **Childcare vouchers/crèche facilities** – some employers offer childcare vouchers which contribute towards childcare costs while employees are at work. Other employers provide a crèche within the workplace for employees' children.

EXAM TIP

Employees choose an employer for a variety of reasons – not just the salary. So additional benefits such as rewards are important in attracting the right candidates to the job.

Employee relations

Businesses try and keep their employees motivated in other ways, too: good team working and staff training, generous holiday allowances, excellent appraisal systems, and involving employees in decision-making can each help to motivate staff. Other businesses go further:

- **Works council** – a committee made up of employees and managers which ensures that employees are consulted and involved in the decision-making process of the business.
- **Quality circles** – groups of employees voluntarily meet to discuss issues for improvement in the business. They focus on production, training and customer service.
- **Employee of the month and achievement awards** – some businesses operate schemes whereby employees can receive awards, bonuses or recognition for performing well.
- **Leisure facilities** – some businesses provide rooms for relaxation or playing games. Some offer reduced price or free gym memberships.

Apply Your Knowledge

Describe how winning an achievement award at school or college would make you feel. List the ways it would make you work harder afterwards.

Develop Your Skills

You are the Human Resources Manager in a large company. Your employees have completed a survey that shows they are not happy at work. Describe how you plan to try and change that.

Quick Test

1. Explain what 'double time' is when paying employees.
2. Define the phrase 'non-financial rewards'.
3. Give two examples of non-financial rewards.
4. Describe the role of a works council.

Trade unions

Trade unions

A trade union is an organisation that employees can join to help them negotiate better terms and conditions. It will advise union members and help resolve disputes with employers; it may also offer additional benefits to its members such as financial services or legal advice.

Industrial action

In an industrial dispute, when no agreement can be reached between the employer and the trade union, industrial action can take place. There are different types of industrial action, some of which are more damaging than others. All forms of industrial action penalise the business but employees can also suffer.

- **Strike** – employees refuse to work but do not get paid.
- **Overtime ban** – employees refuse to work overtime and lose overtime pay.
- **Sit-in** – employees occupy the premises and work cannot take place.
- **Work to rule** – employees only do exactly what their contracts state. Goodwill is lost and some overtime payments may be lost.
- **Go slow** – employees still carry out their work but do it slowly leading to reduced productivity.

No matter what method of industrial action employees take, they won't be paid when they are not working.

There can be positive benefits resulting from industrial action; for example, new procedures can be introduced that employees are happy with.

Apply Your Knowledge

Explain whether you think strikes work. If employees go on strike they will lose pay – the employer may be happy about that. But what about the customers of the business? Describe who you think wins or loses when employees go on strike.

Develop Your Skills

Learn more about trade unions by going to the website of the Trade Union Congress (www.tuc.org.uk). There is information about joining a trade union and employees' rights at work.

Quick Test

1. What is a trade union and what does it do?
2. Why does industrial action sometimes take place?
3. What is the difference between a strike and a sit-in?

Legislation

Legislation

EXAM TIP

You are not expected to know these laws in detail but you are expected to have a basic understanding of what the law is trying to do.

There are a number of laws that have to be followed by both employers and employees. These laws are designed to make the working environment safe and to ensure that employees are treated fairly in the workplace.

Health and Safety at Work Act 1974

This act outlines the responsibilities of both employers and employees in relation to health and safety at work. Employers have a duty to:

* provide and maintain safety equipment and safe systems of work
* ensure materials used are properly stored, handled, used and transported
* provide information, training, instruction and supervision
* provide a safe place of employment, for example, fire extinguishers and protective clothing
* have health and safety representatives.

Employees have a duty to:

* take reasonable care of the health and safety of themselves and of others who may be affected by what they do or do not do
* co-operate with the employer on health and safety matters.

The Equality Act 2010

This act bans unfair treatment and helps achieve equal opportunities in the workplace and in the wider society. It brings together previous acts that deal with discrimination and makes it unlawful to discriminate against anyone on the grounds of:

* sex
* race
* marital status
* religion and belief
* disability
* sexual orientation
* pregnancy.

Any employee who feels that they have been discriminated against under any of these categories may have a case against their employer.

The Freedom of Information Act 2000

This act allows the general public access to information held by public bodies such as the Government and local authorities. It is designed to build trust in the Government since the public know that they can ask for information at any time. Information can come from schools, hospitals, the police, local councils and other public bodies.

The Data Protection Act 1998

This act allows individuals to have access to information about themselves. Any company or organisation that wants to hold data must apply to the Data Protection Registrar. The data must be held according to certain principles, for example, it must be accurate and up-to-date, it must be obtained fairly and lawfully, and it must be protected against misuse.

National Minimum Wage and National Living Wage regulations

Both the National Minimum Wage and National Living Wage were designed and introduced so that people are not paid at the poverty level. The rate for both is set by the Government.

The National Minimum Wage is the least amount you should be paid as a school leaver.

The National Living Wage is paid to those over the age of 25. It is higher than the minimum wage.

Apply Your Knowledge

Why do you think employees could be discriminated against in the workplace? Explain your reasons.

Develop Your Skills

Log onto www.hse.gov.uk and find the current statistics for accidents and days lost from work.

Quick Test

1. Describe the duties of employees under the Health and Safety at Work Act.
2. Explain two ways that employees may be discriminated against at work.
3. Describe two features of the Data Protection Act.

Using ICT to increase efficiency in managing people

Psychometric electronic testing

Many businesses now ask potential employees to complete online aptitude tests or personality tests, often called psychometric tests. The candidate will complete a series of questions online. The results are analysed and the employer then chooses who to interview on the basis of the test results. This can save time since candidates who are unsuitable will not be called for interview.

Psychometric tests can be adapted to suit the requirements of the employer. For example, the police, army and navy each have different tests in comparison to childcare providers.

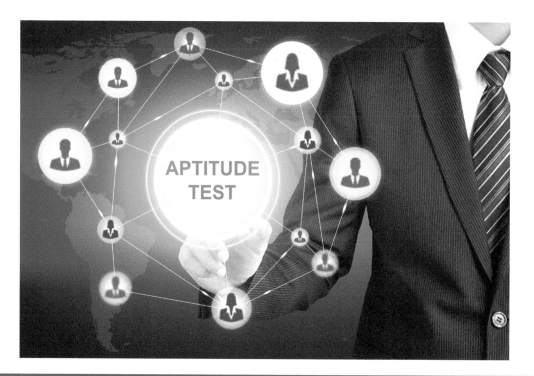

Recruitment and electronic application forms

Employers use websites to advertise job vacancies and manage the recruitment process. The main recruitment websites are used by candidates and employers. In Scotland some of the most popular websites are:

- www.s1jobs.com
- www.myjobscotland.gov.uk
- www.scotcareers.co.uk
- www.monster.co.uk

All of these websites allow applicants to set up their own accounts and store their personal details and CVs. This means that they do not have to re-enter the same information every time they want to apply for a job. The websites carry hundreds of job vacancies; candidates are emailed when jobs are advertised that match their profiles. Many of the websites offer advice on interview techniques and completing job applications.

When candidates apply online for a particular job, they either complete a standard application form or they can upload their CV. Interviews are arranged by email or telephone.

Employee records

Database management systems allow employers to hold up-to-date records about their employees and their service history. Personal information is kept in a database with details of promotions and training undertaken, along with current salary.

Electronic training resources

Both existing and new employees require ongoing training. Many organisations have developed electronic training resources for this purpose. Examples include:

- online videos
- E-learning courses with tests at each stage of training, and interactive resources
- DVDs.

These electronic resources give the employee flexibility to learn at a time and place of their own choosing. They also reduce the amount of time spent away from the workplace and enable employers to provide training of a good standard at a reasonable cost.

Apply Your Knowledge

1. Prepare your own CV by using the suggested headings in the job websites listed on page 81.

2. What do you think are the main skills that employers are looking for in young people?

Develop Your Skills

1. Log onto the recruitment websites listed on page 81 and search for jobs in your local area or a location that interests you. Read the information provided about the jobs.

2. Log onto any website that carries out psychometric tests. Test yourself to see what type of career you might be suited to.

Quick Test

1. Explain how online testing can save time for employers recruiting candidates.

2. Describe the advantages to employers of online applications.

Sources of finance: 1

Sources of finance for the private sector

Businesses need finance to start up and keep going. A range of sources are available to suit different purposes.

Source of finance	Description	Suitable for...
Loan/gift from family or friends	Family or friends may provide a business with finance, and this may not need to be paid back.	Sole trader Partnership
Capital from owners	The owners provide their own finance, for example, from their personal savings or a redundancy payment.	Sole trader Partnership Private limited company
Bank loan	Finance can be borrowed from a bank and repaid with interest. The payments are agreed for a fixed period.	Sole trader Partnership Private limited company
Bank overdraft	The bank allows the business to take more out of a current account than is in it (a negative balance).	Sole trader Partnership Private limited company (for short periods of time)
Government grants	Finance can be obtained from the Government if the business meets certain criteria. Grants do not have to be repaid.	Sole trader Partnership Private limited company
Prince's Trust	For entrepreneurs aged 18–30, the Prince's Trust can provide: (a) low interest start-up loans of up to £5000; (b) small start-up business grants in special circumstances	Sole trader
Shares	The business can issue more shares to shareholders in order to raise more finance.	Private limited company
Mortgage	This can be obtained from a bank or building society and is usually used to buy property over a long period of time.	Sole trader Partnership Private limited company

Source of finance	Description	Suitable for...
Hire purchase	This can be used to obtain equipment and machinery. Payments are made over an agreed period of time, but the equipment does not belong to the business until the final payment has been made.	Sole trader Partnership Private limited company

EXAM TIP

Not all businesses are financed in the same way. It depends on how much finance they need and for how long.

Apply Your Knowledge

If you were starting up in business as a sole trader what would be your preferred sources of finance? Give reasons for your choice.

Develop Your Skills

Log onto www.scottishenterprise.com to find out how businesses in Scotland can obtain funding.

Quick Test

1. Name three sources of finance for a sole trader.
2. Explain what a bank overdraft is.
3. Describe what a mortgage is usually given for.

Sources of finance: 2

Sources of finance for the public sector

Public sector organisations obtain their finance in a different way. The Government collects income tax and other forms of taxation, for example, road tax, corporation tax and VAT. The Government then distributes this income allocating amounts to healthcare, welfare, transport, etc. In Scotland, funding for some services (such as education) is decided by the Scottish Parliament.

Sources of finance for the third sector

Third sector finance is not fixed, and changes depending on how well the economy is performing, and how much grant funding is available from the Government and other sources, such as European Union funding.

Type of finance	Source
Gift finance	Donations from individuals, businesses, sponsorship, the National Lottery, legacies, fundraising activities.
Grant funding	Government, local authorities, enterprise companies, Prince's Trust, European Union.
Trading activities	Charity shops, social enterprises, cafes.

Apply Your Knowledge

Find out why the Government gives grants to businesses in certain areas of the country.

Develop Your Skills

Find out more about the way in which the UK Government spends income from taxation at www.gov.uk/government/collections/national-statistics-release. Here you can see a breakdown of the amount spent on different areas of the economy.

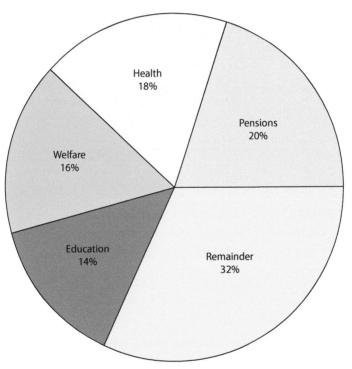

Total UK spending in 2012: £715 billion

Health 18%

Pensions 20%

Welfare 16%

Education 14%

Remainder 32%

Quick Test

1. How does the Government obtain finance for spending on the economy?
2. What is VAT?
3. Identify one method of obtaining finance in the third sector.

Costs and the break-even point

Types of cost

Costs are the bills that businesses need to pay on a regular basis. Some of these costs change regularly while others change rarely.

Fixed costs

Fixed costs are the bills a business has to pay that **do not change** according to output. The important point about fixed costs is that they always have to be paid. Examples of fixed costs are the rent of a factory, the manager's salary and council tax.

Variable costs

Variable costs are the business's bills and expenses **that do change** according to output. The more a business produces, the higher its variable costs will be. Examples of variable costs are raw materials, wages, electricity and gas.

Total costs

For a business, the total cost of production is the fixed costs plus the variable costs. Once all these costs have been calculated then a business can see if it is making a profit or loss.

> **EXAM TIP**
> Fixed costs do not change as output changes. They always have to be paid.

> **EXAM TIP**
> Variable costs rise or fall according to output.

> **EXAM TIP**
> Total costs = fixed costs + variable costs.

Break-even point

The **break-even point** is the point at which sales revenue and total costs are equal and the business is neither making a profit nor a loss.

Calculating profit

Profits are made just above the break-even point. This is the point at which sales revenue is higher than total costs.

Break-even graph

The break-even point can be shown very clearly on a graph. This is a useful tool for analysing sales and costs.

TR = total revenue, TC = total costs, FC = fixed costs. The break-even point is where the TR and TC lines cross.

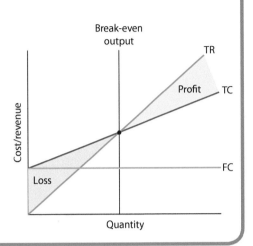

Apply Your Knowledge

Businesses that are starting up often forget about fixed costs. What do you think businesses should do to make sure that they cover their fixed costs?

Develop Your Skills

The break-even point can be calculated using a spreadsheet. Find out how to enter data into a spreadsheet to calculate the break-even point.

Quick Test

1. Describe fixed costs.
2. Describe variable costs.
3. Give one example of a fixed cost and one example of a variable cost.
4. Explain the break-even point.

Cash budgeting

Cashflow

A business has to ensure it has enough cash coming in on a regular basis to be able to pay its bills on time. This is called **cashflow**. A business needs good cashflow otherwise it risks going into liquidation (going bankrupt). Some businesses fail because they run out of cash. Customers may have been given credit for too long, but over this time a business still has to pay its bills. Businesses must anticipate periods when they could run out of cash and take action to deal with this.

A cash budget

This is a financial plan, for example planning for the next three to six months. A cash budget identifies the expected bills and expenses for the business, and the projected revenue or income from sales. A sample cash budget is shown below.

Rosco Ltd cash budget	January	February	March
Opening balance (£)	1000	2900	2000
Cash in			
Sales (£)	13 000	9000	8000
Total in (£)	*14 000*	*11 900*	*10 000*
Cash out			
Purchases of stock (£)	9000	8000	8500
Wages (£)	1000	1000	1000
Electricity (£)	600	500	450
Gas (£)	500	400	400
Total out (£)	*11 100*	*9900*	*10 350*
Closing balance (£)	**2900**	**2000**	**−350**

The closing balance is −£350 in March. It is a projection into the future, but we can see that this *will* happen if the business owner does not take some preventative action.

Cashflow problems and how to solve them

The cash budget will let the owner(s) of a business see forthcoming cashflow problems. Cashflow problems can be solved by one or more of the following: obtaining a loan or an overdraft from the bank; raising extra capital; cutting back on projected expenses; asking suppliers or creditors for extra time to pay bills; spreading the cost of assets, for example, by hire purchase or leasing; cutting down on purchases of stock, for example, by finding a cheaper supplier; encouraging customers to pay on time, for example, by offering discounts.

Generating and spending cash

Businesses generate **cash** by selling goods and services. Payments are received from customers in the form of cash, cheques, credit card payments or bank transfers. This is referred to as 'cash in' or 'money in'. Some sales to customers are made on a **credit** basis. This means that the customers receive the goods immediately, but that the payment for them follows later (for example, after one month).

All businesses have bills to pay. This is referred to as 'cash out' or 'money out'. For instance, businesses have to pay for raw materials, or for the goods they are going to sell to their customers; this is referred to as stock. In addition, businesses have to pay for electricity and gas, insurance, wages, petrol, mobile phones, etc. Some suppliers allow businesses one month to pay their bills.

Apply Your Knowledge

1. What are the main causes of cashflow problems in a business?

2. Why is it necessary to prepare a cash budget?

Develop Your Skills

Enter the figures from the cash budget on page 90 into a spreadsheet and use the formula function to work out the closing balances. Try changing some of the figures for expenses and sales and see how the closing balance figures change.

Quick Test

1. Give two advantages of preparing a cash budget.
2. Identify two expenses for a business.
3. Describe two ways in which a business could solve cashflow problems.
4. Explain how a spreadsheet can help to improve cashflow.

Income statement

Income statement

All businesses have to prepare statements to show how much profit or loss they are making. This will differ in complexity for different types of businesses, but the most common statement is an **income statement**. This is prepared by a business that buys in finished products and sells them to make a profit.

The income statement shows the gross and net profits made by a business. Gross profit is the profit made from buying and selling. Net profit is the profit made after all the expenses of the business have been deducted. An example is shown below.

Income statement		
Sales (£)		230 000
Less cost of sales (£)		125 000
Gross profit (£)		**105 000**
Less expenses		
Mobile phones (£)	1200	
Insurance (£)	2500	
Wages (£)	32 000	
Electricity (£)	2400	
Petrol (£)	2500	
Total expenses (£)		**40 600**
Net profit (£)		**64 400**

EXAM TIP

Gross profit is made from buying and selling finished goods. Net profit is made after all the expenses of the business have been deducted.

The business must be able to identify the reasons for profits and losses. In the income statement above, the business has made a net profit of £64 400. However, if expenses rise or sales fall, this profit will be reduced. In this case, does the business have to reduce unnecessary expenses or do they have to increase the selling price of their products? There may be more than one solution to the problem.

Identifying reasons for loss

The business has to analyse the income statement and decide how to act if a loss has been made. There are several things a business can do to improve their financial position.

- Check on expenses – Are there any expenses which are too high?
- Check on sales – Has the amount of sales revenue decreased, and if so why?
- Check on the cost of sales – Has the amount paid for stock increased, and if so why? Can stock be purchased cheaper somewhere else?

Apply Your Knowledge

How do businesses increase their profits? They have bills to pay but cannot always rely on sales increasing. How do they survive when business conditions are difficult?

Develop Your Skills

Enter the figures from the income statement on page 92 into a spreadsheet. Insert formulae in the appropriate cells. Alter some of the expenses and see how the gross and net profit figures change.

Quick Test

1. Describe what gross profit is.
2. Describe what net profit is.

Using ICT to increase efficiency in finance

Spreadsheets

The finance functions in a business can be enhanced through the use of software and accounting packages. Software can be used to produce customer invoices using a mail-merge function. An accounting package can record transactions and produce income statements that enable the business manager(s) to monitor their financial performance. Spreadsheets can be used to prepare cash budgets and manage cashflow. These tools allow business managers to answer questions such as:

- Which customers still have outstanding bills to pay, and how much are they in total?
- How much cash is in the bank account?
- What was the profit last year compared to this year?
- What is the total cost of expenses, and where do cutbacks need to be made?

Online banking

The growth in the use of online banking has led to businesses encouraging customers to pay their bills online. Customers are given the sort code and account number of the bank account for the business so that payments can be made by online bank transfers.

EPOS

EPOS allows businesses to track their stock accurately. Each item of stock is given a barcode which is scanned when a customer purchases that item; this updates the stock record for that item. Some EPOS systems can also automatically order new stock as and when required.

Apply Your Knowledge

Why would a business manager use a spreadsheet? How could a spreadsheet be used to prepare a cash budget? Think about the formulae you would need to calculate the closing balance each month.

Develop Your Skills

Do you use QR codes? Find out if your smartphone has a QR code reader and how you can use it to access information more quickly.

Quick Test

1. Describe two ways that spreadsheets can be used to help business managers.
2. List two ways that businesses can use technology to train employees.

Quick Test Answers

Satisfying wants (page 15)

1. **Describe the difference between needs and wants.**
   Needs are things we must have, such as food and clothing; wants are things we would like to have, such as cars and computers.

2. **Describe how wealth is created by a business.**
   Wealth is created by a business by adding value at each stage of production, for example, a furniture-maker adds value by creating a table from trees that have been cut down.

Sectors of industry and the economy (page 17)

1. **Name the three sectors of industry.**
   Primary, secondary and tertiary.

2. **Give an example of an organisation that operates in the public sector.**
   Schools, hospitals, council-run leisure centres.

What is customer service? (page 19)

1. **Describe two ways that businesses can offer customers good service.**
   Staff-training, loyalty cards, bonus offers, setting service standards, offering guarantees.

2. **Give three reasons for offering good customer service.**
   Increased customer loyalty, increased sales and profits, a good reputation, increased competitiveness, increased staff morale and effectiveness.

3. **Explain why it is important to train staff in customer service.**
   So that all staff treat customers in the same way and a standard can be set. Nothing is left to chance. So that staff are confident in their ability to deal with customers.

How to maximise customer service (page 21)

1. **Explain the drawbacks of offering guarantees to customers.**
   The business must make sure that it can carry out the terms of the guarantee, otherwise customers will not be happy.

2. **How can a business make sure that customers' complaints are handled correctly?**
   By having a published complaints procedure so that customers know what to do. Also by training staff.

3. **What should a business do if customers are constantly complaining?**
   Make sure that staff are properly trained. Look at the quality of the products or services to see if they need improved. Carry out market research to identify the problem.

Private sector businesses and local government organisations (page 23)

1. **Explain the difference between limited and unlimited liability.**
   Limited liability means that an investor in a business can only lose the share that they have put in if the company goes bankrupt. Unlimited liability means that the owner can also lose all their personal possessions if the business goes bankrupt. For example, a sole trader has unlimited liability.

2. **Describe the ownership of a private limited company.**
   A private limited company is owned by shareholders. However, shares are not available to buy on the stock exchange.

3. **Describe how profits are distributed in a partnership.**
   Profits are split among partners according to the ratio they agreed in the original partnership agreement.

The third sector, charities and social enterprises (page 25)

1. **What are the main aims of third sector organisations?**
   They aim to provide advice, support and education for a particular cause or charity. They raise awareness and funding from grants and donations.

2. **Explain why an entrepreneur might start up a social enterprise business.**
   In order to benefit their local community. In order to develop their skills and expertise in an area that they are comfortable with.

What are business objectives? (page 27)

1. **Describe two objectives of a private sector business.**
   To make a profit, to survive, to grow, to provide a good product or service.

2. **Describe the main objective of public sector organisations.**
   To provide a service to the public.

3. **Describe two objectives of third sector organisations.**
   To provide advice and support to the local community. To raise awareness of a particular cause.

4. **Describe how a social enterprise differs from a private limited company.**
   A social enterprise is primarily concerned with helping the community and although it can make a profit there are no shareholders. A private limited company has shareholders and a board of directors appointed to run the company on behalf of the shareholders.

Factors that affect a business: 1 (page 29)

1. **Describe how the Government can affect the day-to-day running of a business.**
   The Government can introduce laws that affect every business in the UK. Businesses have to comply with these laws and this usually costs them money.

2. **Apart from bad weather, list the other environmental factors that can affect a business.**
   Pollution, and waste disposal, recycling.

got it? ☐ ☐ ☐

Factors that affect a business: 2 (page 31)

1. **Explain the difference between internal and external factors.**
   Internal factors are events and situations *within* the business that affect its performance overall. External factors are *outwith* the business.
2. **Give the actions a business must take if it installs new technology.**
   The business must ensure that the technology is up-to-date and that all staff are trained in the use of the technology.

Stakeholders: 1 (page 33)

1. **Name two internal and two external stakeholders.**
   Internal – owners (including shareholders), employees, managers
   External – customers, suppliers, banks, the local community (including pressure groups), the Government.
2. **What interest does the local community have in a business?**
   The local community will want jobs provided and also want the community to be free from pollution.
3. **What interest does the Government have in a business?**
   The Government is interested in the business paying tax and keeping within the law.

Stakeholders: 2 (page 35)

1. **Outline actions that employees can take which may affect a business.**
   Employees can choose to work hard and deliver products and services of good quality. They can also take industrial action.
2. **Describe the consequences for a business if they have to change supplier.**
   They may have to pay higher prices or accept goods of inferior quality.
3. **Describe the main actions that customers can take if they are not happy with a business.**
   Go to another business, complain, spread the word to other customers that they are not happy.

Who are your customers? (page 37)

1. **Explain why businesses need to know who their customers are.**
   So that they can target their customers by producing goods and services that they want.

2. **What is meant by market segments?**
   Specific groups of people in the market who all want similar things, for example, teenagers.

3. **Why is it important to target specific market segments?**
   To avoid wasting resources and to make sure that products get to the correct market segment.

4. **What products would you aim at children aged 5–8 years?**
   Toys, books, DVDs, sweets, electronic games, bicycles, etc.

Market research: 1 (page 39)

1. **Explain what is meant by market research.**
   Finding out what customers want by asking them directly or gathering information from other sources.

2. **How does market research help a business?**
   It helps to know what customers want so that resources are not wasted providing other products.

3. **Why would a researcher carry out an interview instead of a postal survey?**
   To see the facial expression and to get to know the interviewee better.

4. **What is the main benefit of field research?**
   You can get immediate answers to questions and people will be more honest face-to-face.

GOT IT? ▢ ▢ ▢

Market research: 2 (page 41)

1. **What is desk research?**
   Finding information from existing or secondary sources.

2. **Outline two methods of desk research.**
   Using Government statistics that have already been gathered; using websites with relevant information; using books, magazines, etc.

3. **What is the main benefit of desk research?**
   The information is usually available free of charge.

The marketing mix: product (page 45)

1. **Describe three stages of the product development process.**
   An idea is generated. Market research is undertaken. Product research is undertaken. A prototype is developed. The prototype is tested on the market. Adaptations are made on the basis of market testing. The product is launched.

2. **Name the four stages of the product lifecycle.**
   Introduction, growth, maturity and decline.

3. **Suggest two ways that the product lifecycle can be extended.**
   Changing the product in some way, changing the packaging, altering the price, changing the place where it is sold.

The marketing mix: price (page 47)

Name and describe two pricing strategies.
Cost plus pricing, penetration pricing, destroyer pricing.

The marketing mix: place (page 51)

1. **Name the four methods of distributing products to customers.**
   Road, rail, sea and air.

2. **Give one advantage and one disadvantage for each of the methods.**

   Road – products go directly to customers but can be expensive.

   Rail – quick and easy to transport large and bulky items but not always direct to customers if train station is far away from them.

   Sea – useful for very large items e.g. containers, and for overseas, however takes a long time.

   Air – very quick for long distances but very expensive to transport goods.

The marketing mix: promotion (page 53)

1. **Give two methods of promotion.**
   Money-off vouchers, discounts, BOGOF, free samples.

2. **List two methods of advertising.**
   On TV and radio, billboards and posters, in cinemas, newspapers and magazines, by flyers and leaflets, on websites, by email and text messaging, via sponsorship and celebrity endorsements.

Using ICT to increase efficiency in marketing (page 55)

1. **Describe two advantages of electronic surveys for a business.**
   The information from the survey can be gathered quickly and the results can be analysed online. Electronic surveys can be used for both customers and employees; employee satisfaction surveys can be carried out quickly and confidentially.

2. **Describe two advantages of internet advertising.**
   A global audience can be reached on a regular basis. New animation and graphic techniques means that internet adverts look just like TV adverts. Internet advertising can be targeted directly at customers depending on what they are browsing. Internet advertising is professional and eye-catching.

3. **Describe two advantages of online shopping, for both the business and the customer.**
Business – increases sales because of online shopping; easier to target new customers on internet websites.
Customer – a choice of where and when they want to shop; products delivered to their homes; secure online payment systems.

What is operations? (page 57)

1. **Identify three features of a good supplier.**
Delivers on time, has good quality materials, charges good prices.

2. **Explain what just-in-time stock control means.**
Raw materials are delivered just in time for the production process rather than holding large stocks.

3. **Explain what maximum stock means.**
The maximum amount of stock that a business holds at any one time. Usually depends on how much they use and how much storage space they have.

4. **Describe the advantages to a business of using EPOS.**
Stock levels can be monitored easily. Stock can be re-ordered automatically. Stock lists can be printed regularly.

Production (page 59)

1. **Explain the difference between capital-intensive and labour-intensive production.**
Capital-intensive mainly uses machines in the production process;
labour-intensive uses mainly people in the production process.

2. **Identify two examples of products that are made using job production.**
Wedding dresses and birthday cakes.

3. **Describe one advantage and one disadvantage of batch production.**
Advantage – products can be made more cheaply than with job production.
Disadvantage – if there is a problem the whole batch may be wasted.

4. **Explain why products are cheaper to produce using flow production.**
Production volumes are high, therefore the unit costs of production are lower.

Quality (page 61)

1. **Describe two features of a quality product.**
   Quality products should be safe and fit for purpose. They should last for the period of time expected at purchase.

2. **Describe quality assurance.**
   Checking products at more regular intervals during the production process and trying to avoid problems happening in the first place.

3. **Describe quality management.**
   This involves every employee in the organisation ensuring that quality is built-in at each and every stage of the production process.

4. **List the benefits to a business of good quality products.**
   Customers will be happy with the products and will therefore return to buy more. Happy customers will enhance the reputation of the business. Employees will be more satisfied and better motivated. Products of good quality reduce waste. Profits may be increased.

What are ethical and environmental issues?: 1 (page 63)

1. **Explain why it is important for businesses to choose an environmentally friendly supplier.**
   To make sure that any raw materials have been produced or obtained in an ethical way.

2. **Give two main ways in which the environment can be damaged.**
   Greenhouse gas emissions and dumping of waste.

3. **What is sustainable development?**
   When businesses replace raw materials that they are constantly using; for example by replanting trees.

What are ethical and environmental issues?: 2 (page 65)

1. **Give two costs and two benefits of recycling.**
   Costs - providing bins and bags; paying the salaries of personnel who collect, transport and process waste; providing recycling sites.

   Benefits - protecting natural resources, saving energy, protecting the natural environment, fewer landfill sites.

2. **Give one cost and one benefit of reducing packaging.**
   Reducing packaging can increase the risk of products becoming damaged; however, reducing packaging can help protect the environment by reducing waste.

Using ICT to increase efficiency in operations (page 67)

1. **Give a description of CAD.**
   Computer-aided design where software is used in the design process.

2. **Give a description of CAM.**
   Computer-aided manufacture where computers are used in the production process.

3. **Explain EPOS and how it helps with stock control.**
   Electronic point of sale. When products are sold and 'bleeped' through at the checkout, stock levels are automatically updated. This allows reorders of those items to be made.

Recruitment (page 69)

1. **Compare internal and external recruitment.**
   Internal recruitment is when a vacancy is filled from within the business.
   External recruitment is when a vacancy is advertised on the open market and
   the new employee may come from outwith the business.

2. **Identify three pieces of information contained in a job description.**
   Job title, hours of work, rate of pay, holidays, duties and responsibilities.

3. **Describe what a recruitment agency would use a person specification for.**
   To cross-check the skills and qualities of applicants for a job against those in
   the person specification.

4. **Identify three places where jobs can be advertised externally.**
   Internet websites, newspapers, job centres.

Selection of employees (page 71)

1. **Give the advantages of using an interview as the only means of selecting a candidate for a job.**
   The interview can give an in-depth insight into the candidate. Candidates have an
   opportunity to outline their strengths and give details from their experiences.

2. **Describe the disadvantages of using personality tests as a means of selecting candidates.**
   Not all the candidates may fit neatly into the designated categories of
   personality tests. Candidates can be nervous because of the test and give
   unsatisfactory answers. Candidates can be dishonest in their answers.

3. **Describe the role a recruitment agency plays in the recruitment process.**
   The recruitment agency advertises the vacancy on behalf of the business; they
   collect and process applications, checking them against the essential and
   desirable attributes in the person specification; and they arrange the interviews
   and other selection procedures on behalf of the business.

Training of employees (page 73)

1. **Explain the difference between on-the-job and off-the-job training.**
   On-the-job training takes place at the place of work and usually involves demonstrations, job rotation, etc. Off-the-job training involves going to an external training centre and being trained by an expert.

2. **Describe two costs and two benefits of on-the-job training.**
   Costs – time is lost when the employee is at the training; employees may feel awkward being trained by each other.
   Benefits – training is job-specific; no time is spent travelling to and from the training centre.

3. **Describe two methods of employee training that could be done off-the-job.**
   College lectures, role play, multimedia DVDs.

4. **Describe what induction training is.**
   Training that is given to new employees in a business for them to find out about the business and the job.

Motivating and retaining employees (page 75)

1. **Explain what 'double time' is when paying employees.**
   Double time is the rate of hourly pay multiplied by two.

2. **Define the phrase 'non-financial rewards'.**
   These are additional benefits given to employees but not in the form of cash.

3. **Give two examples of non-financial rewards.**
   Company car, pension contributions, luncheon vouchers, childcare vouchers.

4. **Describe the role of a works council.**
   A committee of employees and management that discusses areas of the business they are concerned about so that everyone is working towards the goals of the business.

Trade unions (page 77)

1. **What is a trade union and what does it do?**
   A trade union is an organisation made up of employees in the workplace. It provides help and advice to members and negotiates for better terms and conditions.

2. **Why does industrial action sometimes take place?**
   Because employees and management have a disagreement which they cannot resolve.

3. **What is the difference between a strike and a sit-in?**
   A strike is when employees refuse to attend for work; a sit-in is when employees occupy the workplace and do not go home.

Legislation (page 79)

1. **Describe the duties of employees under the Health and Safety at Work Act.**
   To ensure that they protect themselves and others in the workplace. To ensure that they use any items given to them for health and safety purposes.

2. **Explain two ways that employees may be discriminated against at work.**
   On the grounds of sex, race, religion or disability.

3. **Describe two features of the Data Protection Act.**
   The data must be held according to certain principles, for example it must be accurate and up-to-date, it must be obtained fairly and lawfully and it must be protected against misuse.

Using ICT to increase efficiency in managing people (page 83)

1. **Explain how online testing can save time for employers recruiting candidates.**
   Candidates who are not suitable according to the test do not have to be called for interview.

2. **Describe the advantages to employers of online applications.**
   Applications can be received and processed quickly on the website; this means that shortlisted candidates can be emailed sooner with invitations to interviews.

got it? ▢ ▢ ▢

Quick Test Answers

Sources of finance: 1 (page 85)

1. **Name three sources of finance for a sole trader.**
   Personal savings, family and friends, bank loan.

2. **Explain what a bank overdraft is.**
   A short-term loan from the bank when you are allowed to withdraw more than you have in a bank account. Interest is charged on the overdraft.

3. **Describe what a mortgage is usually given for.**
   The purchase of a property or premises.

Sources of finance: 2 (page 87)

1. **How does the Government obtain finance for spending on the economy?**
   They raise taxes from businesses and individuals.

2. **What is VAT?**
   Value Added Tax – this is added to purchases made by consumers.

3. **Identify one method of obtaining finance in the third sector.**
   Gifts, donations, grants from the Government, trading activities (for example a coffee shop).

Costs and the break-even point (page 89)

1. **Describe fixed costs.**
   Costs that do not change as output changes.

2. **Describe variable costs.**
   Costs that do change as output changes.

3. **Give one example of a fixed cost and one example of a variable cost.**
   Fixed costs – rent, manager's salary, council tax. Variable costs – wages, raw materials.

4. **Explain the break-even point.**
   The point at which neither a profit nor a loss is being made.

109

Cash budgeting (page 91)

1. **Give two advantages of preparing a cash budget.**
    A business can plan its income and expenditure. It can be seen where there may be financial problems in the future.

2. **Identify two expenses for a business.**
    Stationery for the office, rent, telephone bills, electricity, employee wages, etc.

3. **Describe two ways in which a business could solve cashflow problems.**
    Obtaining a loan or an overdraft from the bank. By raising extra capital. By cutting back on projected expenses. By asking suppliers or creditors for extra time to pay bills. By spreading the cost of purchase of assets; for example, through hire purchase or leasing. By cutting down on purchases of stock; for example, by finding a cheaper supplier. By encouraging customers to pay on time; for example, by offering discounts.

4. **Explain how a spreadsheet can help to improve cashflow.**
    Formulae can be entered into a spreadsheet to perform calculations. Changes can be made to data and the formulae will automatically update all the data.

Income statement (page 93)

1. **Describe what gross profit is.**
    Gross profit is the profit made from buying and selling goods and services. It is calculated by subtracting the cost of goods sold from the income gained through sales.

2. **Describe what net profit is.**
    Net profit is gross profit minus the expenses of the business.

Using ICT to increase efficiency in finance (page 95)

1. **Describe two ways that spreadsheets can be used to help business managers.**
    Spreadsheets can be used to prepare cash budgets and manage cashflow allowing business managers to make decisions quickly.

2. **List two ways that businesses can use technology to train employees.**
    Online videos, e-learning courses, DVDs.